The Illustrated History of

TORTURE

From the Roman Empire to the War on Terror

Jack Vernon

CARLTON

CONTENTS

5 Introduction
6 Beating, Whipping, and Stoning
8 Mutilation
10 Flaying
12 Scaphism
14 Frying, Boiling, and Roasting
16 Crucifixion
18 Gladiators
20 Trials by Ordeal
22 Hanging, Drawing, and Quartering
24 Inquisitions
28 Strappado
30 Breaking
32 Cutting and Sawing
34 Crushing
36 Water Tortures
38 Piercing
40 Impalement
42 Witch Hunts
44 Burning and Branding
46 Flogging
48 Wartime Torture
50 Drugs and Psychochemicals
52 Electric Shock Torture
54 Necklacing
56 Psychological Torture
58 Waterboarding
60 Further Reading
61 Notable Dungeons, Torture Chambers, and Museums
62 Index
63 Credits

INTRODUCTION

ABOVE: During the Spanish Inquisition victims might be suspended from the ceiling with weights attached. Eventually the spine would be dislocated and then broken.

Pain is a fundamental survival mechanism. Without pain it becomes more difficult to know what is dangerous to our own survival. We are protected from further danger because fire burns, bruises ache, and a cut stings. And when pain disappears we know that we are getting better.

But this simple mechanism can be abused. This book details the myriad ways that pain and anguish can be inflicted, and the reasons why. Sometimes it is to extract information or a confession. Sometimes it is to coerce someone not to deviate, or to demonstrate to others what will happen if they do so. Sometimes it is to punish or for the purposes of revenge. In some cases it is a

Through a variety of removable items and terrifying images, *The Illustrated History of Torture* explores all aspects of this practice. It includes signed authorizations of torture, a confession by Guy Fawkes extracted through its use, poetry written from the perspective of someone condemned to death, and measures taken to prevent torture such as an Executive Order signed by President Barack Obama. What links all the items, acts and devices in this book is one simple thing: that excruciating pain can be a fate worse

BEATING, WHIPPING, AND STONING

The attitudes of early societies to torture can only be surmised by analyzing the evidence which survives from them. Because pre-Bronze Age societies have left no written records, our knowledge of them depends on the archeological traces left by their settlements. Beating with fists or weapons, stoning, and to a lesser extent whipping, are forms of attack that require much less preparation and thought than many of the others depicted in this book. They are also the earliest forms of torture. Put simply, the difference between torture and any other form of attack is the ability of the target or victim to fight back and defend themselves. If an individual is unable to do so, whether because of their being overwhelmed by superior numbers or physically restrained, then any form of attack can become torture.

Obviously no records exist of this practice from the very earliest times, as any evidence about the nature of injuries found on fossilized human corpses is not specific enough to indicate injuries sustained through torture rather than in combat. Although cave paintings do depict killing, they more often show hunters and animals rather than any human against human violence. Contemporary tribal practices in isolated areas can, however, give us an idea of how beatings may be used, whether in the form of punitive measures or as a rite of passage. Present-day gang initiations and even college hazing also rely on this form of initiation.

ABOVE: In biblical times an angry mob gathers in a courtyard to stone a sinner, although his praying stance suggests he seeks forgiveness.

In ancient cultures, the role of the whip was rather different to that which it later had, as it was used primarily to punish or motivate slaves when they were working. Although the extent to which slavery was used in the construction of great monuments such as the Pyramids of Egypt is unknown, archeologists have calculated that, as well as the skilled workers needed to construct them, there would have to have been a large number of laborers, possibly from as few as 2,000 to as many as 30,000 people. This workforce would have been made up of people from the surrounding countryside and, although they would not have been slaves in the traditional sense, their obligation to the Egyptian hierarchy of "God-kings" would have made refusal to work very difficult indeed. Hence, their labor was a form of slavery, and the whipping a type of torture.

The Egyptian whip probably resembled a contemporary bullwhip. Slaves were regarded as little more than property and, like any other animals, would be lightly whipped to keep them working. The idea that this was torture was far from the mind of the overseers, though punishments frequently involved 1,000 lashes in public.

Stoning had a different significance in ancient societies from how it is viewed today. While it is true that there are many documented instances of crowds or mobs forming and spontaneously stoning criminals or people who had transgressed, it was also a punishment required and legitimized by religious doctrine.

In the Talmud, the sacred Jewish document, stoning was a sanctioned form of execution for 18 crimes, from bestiality to idolatry, and even for cursing a parent. However, these were not thoughtlessly applied, at least by the standards of the time, and any crimes requiring capital punishment had to be heard before a council of Talmudic scholars, with at least two witnesses bearing testament to the transgression. Not all crimes were punishable by stoning, others calling for flogging, hanging, burning, or being put to the sword.

Stoning is also sanctioned in some circumstances by Islamic Sharia law, the principles of which are based on the Koran and the Hadith (sayings associated with the Prophet Muhammad and his companions). However, stoning is not specifically mentioned in the Koran and some Muslims therefore consider it to be an illegitimate punishment. Controversially, it is still practiced to this day in some Middle Eastern countries.

These three forms of torture, although simpler than some of the methods that came later, each symbolize the various roles that torture plays in society, from punitive justice to the controlling of subjects, to simple sadism masked as religious fervor.

ABOVE: St. Anthony is subjected to Bastinado by a group of demonic figures.

Bastinado

Foot whipping, known as bastinado, falaka or phalanga, is a form of torture where the soles of the feet are lashed with a club, a small bullwhip, or a wooden cane. There are large clusters of nerve endings on the foot near the plantar fascia and these can be severely damaged by this torture, inflicting a disproportionate level of agony on the victim. The whip can also break bones and tendons which take a long time to heal, meaning prolonged anguish and walking impairment.

BELOW: This fresco from the tomb of Menna, an Egyptian scribe, depicts a slave being beaten by his master. The third figure, also a slave may be pleading for leniency or simply wishing to be spared the same fate himself. The short whip used here may in fact be made of knotted cords rather than leather.

MUTILATION

While most torture inevitably features some form of mutilation of the human body, it can also be torture to inflict this on the body for its own sake, often with the intention of leaving permanent scars. This particular form of torture depends not only on the pain inflicted, but also on the social impact of the victim's being permanently disabled or disfigured, and therefore suffering ridicule or ostracism.

Two torture devices that often caused mutilation were the stocks and the pillory. These are familiar to contemporary audiences and are usually portrayed in a humorous way, with the victim subjected to nothing worse than the throwing of rotten fruit and vegetables, but the reality was much grimmer. Stocks were ground-level wooden slats into which the legs could be locked, whereas pillories were made up of a slat mounted on a free-standing piece of wood through which both the arms and the head could be secured, if desired, with the victim standing. Those placed into these devices, whether as a punishment for crimes such as theft or violence (or in the case of women for perceived "shrewishness" or adultery), were not just humiliated, but were also extremely vulnerable. Victims could be spat at and urinated and defecated upon, and most ended up suffering horrible mutilation. This, combined with the incredible discomfort and possible starvation, led to some dying in the stocks and pillories.

Another form of mutilation punishment was the removal of specific body parts for committing specific crimes. Tongues would be pulled out from

ABOVE: The pillory was still in use as late as the nineteenth century, as shown in this picture of the Tombs prison in New York City.

LEFT: A man is placed in the pillory for "A seditious libel" in the seventeenth century whilst onlookers point and jeer.

those who uttered blasphemy or nagging wives. The removal of hands from thieves is well documented in both Judaic and Islamic culture. In later history, sometimes even the removal of both hands was practiced, as in the case of Galvarino, a Mapuche warrior captured by the Spanish at the Battle of Lagunillas during the Arauco War of the 1550s. He actually survived and took part in future battles with knives fixed onto the stumps.

Castration was a disturbingly common form of mutilation in ancient cultures. The ancient Egyptians castrated captured enemies, then forced them into slavery as eunuchs (although those in the royal household often achieved positions of great power). These eunuchs would then be used as household workers and attendants for women, as they were considered trustworthy because of the stifling of their sexual desires. In later cultures, castrati were considered to be a "third sex," and famed for their abilities to sing incredibly

ABOVE: An anonymous engraving portraying mutilation being performed during the Great Witch Trial of Schongau, which took place in Bavaria in the sixteenth century.

LEFT: Prologue of the Hammurabi code on a clay tablet, currently held at the Louvre in Paris.

BELOW: Galvarino the Mapuche warrior standing defiantly despite his amputated hands.

Circumcision has been practiced in many cultures, and while debates on whether male circumcision counts as mutilation or is a biological necessity continue to rage, it is generally agreed that female circumcision, more accurately called female genital mutilation, is unnecessary. Practiced by some early cultures as a form of sexual repression and as part of religious ceremonies, circumcisions would naturally be performed without any form of anaesthetic (as none existed) and the process was incredibly painful and dangerous.

Judicial and social practices in Egypt and Babylon (and many other ancient cultures) could prescribe the removal of almost any body part, and the humiliating and possibly crippling nature of the injuries inflicted, while not necessarily fatal, would make the rest of the individual's life a form of torture. The mutilation of bodies after death was also sometimes practiced as a way of denying individuals satisfaction in the afterlife, and, while to our culture this does not necessarily represent torture, it was enacted with the intention of inflicting it.

The Code of Hammurabi

Hammurabi was the sixth king of Babylon (from 1792 BC to 1750 BC). At the time in Babylon the sentences passed (and the punishments inflicted) for crimes varied widely, so at his behest the Code of Hammurabi was created, consisting of 282 laws set out on 12 tablets. The laws were a complex extension of the eye-for-an-eye principle, with each punishment directly mirroring the crime, so an arsonist would be set on fire, and a son guilty of striking a father had his hand cut off.

FLAYING

ABOVE: Tezcatlipoca consuming the palm of a sacrificed prisoner. The heads surrounding him represent his power over the 13 days of the Aztec calendar.

Flaying is one of the earliest recorded forms of torture. Its emergence parallels the development of knives, particularly their use for the skinning and wearing of animal skins for warmth. In fact, some cultures used human skin in the same way, occasionally regarding it as more desirable than animal skin because of the significance of its having been obtained through the defeat of an enemy.

Examples of flaying are common in almost all cultures, particularly ancient ones that had not developed more sophisticated torture equipment. The Assyrians in particular used it both as a punishment and as a form of political action during their campaigns of conquest in the Middle East in the first half of the first millennium BC. A captured enemy, sometimes a leader, would be flayed and their skin nailed up on the wall of their home city as a warning to others.

In Aztec culture, flaying was a religious practice, with many victims subjected to it as a sacrifice to Xipe Totec (also known as Tezcatlipoca), the flayed god of life, death, and rebirth. Flaying is also mentioned in Greek mythology as the fate of Marsyas the satyr for failing in a music contest with Apollo. Afterward, his skin was nailed to a pine tree.

Mentions of flaying in the bible are rare, but include Leviticus 1:6—"And he shall flay the burned offering, and cut it into his pieces." The offering in question is presumably here not human. The most famous occurrence of flaying in the Catholic tradition is that of Bartholomew the Apostle, but the story may be apocryphal.

The techniques of flaying, although they varied in different cultures, tended to conform to certain standard practices. The victim would usually be hung upside down, sometimes crucified with the limbs fixed by ropes or metal bands, and incisions would be made at key points, around the neck and arm joints. Then, slowly the blade would be applied under the skin and pulled away from the body. This torture would not only cause the agony of having the nerve endings torn away from the flesh, but would also expose the raw muscular structure to the elements. Once the stomach was reached, the intestines would fall out, causing even greater agony. Flaying was not a form of torture used to extract information, but was employed as a punishment before death or as an example to others.

Of course, there were ways to use flaying that did not lead to the death of the victim, such as flaying only certain parts of their anatomy. In particularly cruel cultures, such as that of Assyria, the victim could be flayed while a friend or family member (often a child) watched.

This form of torture remained popular throughout history, owing to its painfulness and the brutal significance of treating the victim like an animal.

ABOVE: A ritual sacrifice to Tezcatlipoca atop a Ziggurat as part of a festival.

BELOW: Marsyas the satyr of Greek legend, restrained prior to his flaying.

Sometimes corpses would even be flayed after death as a way of denying the victim entrance to the afterlife, or so that the torturer could use the skin for magical purposes. Native Americans became infamous for their habit of scalping victims, removing only the skin on the head, but in reality it was not a practice in widespread use among tribes. In fact, white hunters were far more likely to employ it as a form of retaliation, and also to claim bounties on the scalps.

Whatever the purpose of flaying, there is no denying its power both to punish the victim and horrify anyone who learns of it.

St Bartholomew the Apostle

Although he is one of the 12 apostles, information on St. Bartholomew is scarce. The Christian writer Eusebius recorded him as teaching in India (at that time India was a term used to indicate a much wider series of lands, including Arabia) and a great number of religious texts and portraits depict him as having been flayed alive and crucified upside-down in Albanopolis in Armenia by Astyages, for having converted his brother, King Polymius. In statues, Bartholomew often holds his flayed skin draped over his arm.

SCAPHISM

Although all torture is abhorrent, and many of those featured in this book are sadistic in the extreme, scaphism is arguably one of the most horrific—albeit creative—forms of torture ever invented. It originated in Persia around 400 BC, but was used only rarely then, as even by the standards of the time it was particularly cruel and unpleasant.

Scaphism (from the greek "skaphe," meaning hollowed or scooped out) is also known as "the boats," because it involves the victim being placed into one boat, while another is inverted on top to enclose him within, with holes cut for his limbs and head. The boats could also be hollowed out logs, hence the etymology of the name.

The victim would then be fed milk and honey, forcefully if they resisted, and be slathered in the mixture. After a while this would cause involuntary bowel movements and diarrhea. They would be forced to lie in this filth, inducing further sickness and discomfort.

At this point, the victim would be floated out to the center of a lake or some other body of water and left. Inevitably, insects such as flies, wasps, and

ABOVE: The Battle of Cunaxa, fought between two brothers, Cyrus the Younger and Artaxerxes, in 401 BC. Cyrus' killer Mithridates was executed by scaphism

RIGHT: Cyrus' head and hands were paraded through the battlefield along with those of his slain commanders.

horseflies would gather around, attracted by the scent of the food substances and waste matter, and would begin to feast on both those and the victim's body, causing immeasurable agony. As the process advanced, the victim could be drawn back to the shore, forcibly fed again, and then pushed back out to continue being consumed alive. Victims were said to have been maintained in this state for many days, their bodies slowly devoured, until they eventually died of a combination of sunstroke, organ failure, and blood poisoning. The sight of a victim executed in this manner would be horrifying, and it is assumed that part of the appeal of this extreme form of torture must have been the cautionary nature of its application.

While accounts of this specific punishment are scarce—hopefully because it was not considered to be necessary too often—similar punishments are documented in other societies.

Native Americans would smear captives in honey or some other sweet substance and leave them tied to the ground, or buried up to their neck. While this was commonly depicted in Western films, unlike many other practices

BELOW: Blowfly larvae, from the family Calliphoridae. These maggots hatch from eggs that are usually laid in batches of 150–200, then burrow into rotten or septic flesh using their mouth hooks, which is most unpleasant for the victim.

Mithridates (died 401 BC)

Mithridates was a Persian soldier whose only historical notability is that according to Plutarch in his *Life of Artaxerxes*, he accidentally shot and killed Cyrus the Younger, a Persian prince and army commander. Mithridates then stupidly boasted in the court about this act and was sentenced to scaphism. It is said he survived for 17 days, repeatedly being brought back to the shore and kept alive with food and water. This seemed to the Persians to be appropriate for his crime, even though it was an accidental one.

attributed to "Red Indians" this one was not apocryphal, although it was more commonly inflicted on enemy tribesmen than on any captured white settlers.

There were also other devices designed to force the victim to stew in their own filth, such as the barrel pillory, also known as the Spanish mantle, which was quite literally a barrel in to which the victim was fixed, their head secured at the top and their legs at the bottom, and then paraded around and humiliated. This was also known as the drunkard's cloak, owing to its use in some European countries as a punishment for wayward drunkenness.

Other outdoor tortures often employ the attack of insects as a component, such as crucifixion, breaking on the wheel, and being placed in an iron cage. Although the latter became common during later medieval and Renaissance cultures, it is likely the conditions that those captured in battle were kept in were unpleasant and unhygienic. Therefore, although scaphism is the deliberate use of the principal of being consumed by insects, similar yet less elaborate tortures in ancient cultures might have been carried out by simply not regarding the health and well being of those held captive.

FRYING, BOILING, AND ROASTING

To cultures like those of the Greeks and Romans that adored food and prized the elaborate preparations involved, employing culinary-related techniques to torture people must have seemed amusingly ironic. These practices also cast the victim in the role of an animal, a human sacrifice in an age when the literal sacrifice of humans to the gods had been abandoned as being uncivilized. It cannot be coincidental that the most common use of these forms of torture in Roman culture was in the persecution of Jews and Christians, both groups which rejected the notion of physical sacrifice to the gods.

Although frying, boiling, and roasting all employ different torture techniques, the pain they generated would be similar; the choice of which method to be used was probably more dependent on the type of spectacle that needed to be created.

One of the most infamous historical accounts of these tortures is the story of Hannah and her seven sons, which is related in the biblical book of Maccabees. The sons were seized by the Seleucid ruler Antiochus IV and ordered to consume pork, a practice forbidden by Judaism, to show their allegiance to him. When they refused "...the king being angry commanded frying-pans, and brazen cauldrons to be made hot: which forthwith being heated, he commanded to cut out the tongue of him that had spoken first: and the skin of his head being drawn off, to chop off also the extremities of his hands and feet, the rest of his brethren, and his mother, looking on. And when he was now maimed in all parts, he commanded him...to be fried in the frying-pan: and while he was suffering therein long torments, the rest, together with the mother, exhorted one another to die manfully..."

Each of the brothers was similarly tortured to death and the story became a popular subject of later medieval mystery plays, which went into elaborate, almost excessive, detail about each of the killings, including almost every method of torture known and even some unusual ones, like the idea of being crushed in a giant pestle and mortar. It is thought the word "macabre" derives from a corruption of the

LEFT: St. Cecilia was sentenced to death by "suffocation by steam" but when this failed she was stabbed.

The Brazen Bull of Phalaris

Legend has it, the first victim of this ancient Greek torture device was its designer Perillos of Athens. Perillos's creation was an ornate bull made of brass, into which the victim was fixed. A fire was lit underneath and through a special design their screams were transmuted into melodious bellowing. He presented it to the tyrannical Phalaris, ruler of Acragas in Sicily. Phalaris then suggested Perillos climb inside to demonstrate. The test proved all too successful. However, other legends suggest that Phalaris himself was later subjected to the bull.

ABOVE: "Punishment of one of the women of the king of Juida and her lover." "Juida" is Ouidah in Dahomey, West Africa (now Benin). Her lover is roasted alive while she is buried, in view of an enormous crowd of the King's subjects.

LEFT: Pierre Woeiriot's sketch entitled *Perillus Condemned to the Bronze Bull by Phalaris.*

Latin "Machabaeorum chorea," which translates as dance of the Maccabees, although this is not certain.

Boiling in cauldrons could be done either with water, or with oil, which has a higher boiling point than water and would therefore inflict even more pain. Oil is also more viscous than water and would be more likely to cling to the victim causing further agony. Although not frequently used in early Roman history, as the persecution of Christians grew it became increasingly common. In AD 64, the Emperor Nero infamously sentenced large numbers of Christians to all sorts of horrifying tortures in revenge for their alleged role in a fire that devastated the city of Rome. These included being dipped in wax and oil and burned as torches. He is also said to have had St. John the Apostle boiled alive in a cauldron, although the saint allegedly miraculously escaped unharmed.

Roasting victims, as opposed to directly setting them on fire, was less common, beyond showy ornate devices like the "Brazen Bull." However it did take place, sometimes with the victim suspended over the fire on a rope, or turning on a spit in a cruel imitation of a roast boar. On occasion, fire was not necessary, and in Greek culture people could be roasted to death through exposure to the sun, being tied into a sack and simply left there.

The psychological impact of these tortures to the witnesses and the victim, with the sound and smell that accompanied them, must have been incredible.

CRUCIFIXION

ABOVE: The Crucifixion of St. Peter, painted in 1426 by Italian Renaissance artist Masaccio. It's generally accepted that Peter personally requested that he be crucified upside-down as he didn't consider himself worthy to die the same way as his savior. However it's very unusual for the victim to be able to choose the method of their death.

No torture has had such a transformation of significance as crucifixion, changing from the favored Roman form of punishment for thieves and traitors to an act heralded by Christians as a supreme representation of self-sacrifice for the good of humankind. In contemporary culture, the crucifix is a symbol of hope worn by millions of Christians, despite the reality of its brutal impact (or perhaps because of it). Some Catholic statuary of Christ suffering on the cross almost celebrates the gory nature of this punishment.

The act of being fixed onto a standing object and left to die was not a form of torture used exclusively by the Romans. Norse legend in the *Hávámal* speaks of Odin being hung on a tree for nine days and nights as a sacrifice to himself, and this no doubt echoed notions at the time of holy sacrifice and punishment.

Other ancient peoples who practiced crucifixion included the Scythians, Iranian horse-people of the steppe, the Persians, the Phoenicians, the Carthaginians, and the Greeks. In fact, in Greek culture the idea of crucifixion

St. Andrew

St. Andrew was a Galilean Fisherman who, with his brother Simon Peter, became one of the 12 apostles. After the death of Christ, he was said to have traveled widely, preaching and converting many, but accounts of his life tell that he was crucified as a Christian martyr in the city of Patras on the coast of the Peloponnese. Legend has it he requested to be put onto an X-shaped cross so as not to die the same way as Christ. This version has in consequence become known as a St. Andrew cross and features on the Scottish flag.

RIGHT: Christ on the cross, central panel of a triptych painted in the sixteenth century by Merten Van Heemskerck. A Roman soldier pierces his side with a spear. Visual depictions of Jesus' death are myriad and differ according to the artist's interests and the time they were painted, as well as disagreements in doctrine.

did not just apply to the act of being fixed onto a pole or cross-beam, but also to being impaled onto a spike. That the pain inflicted by the latter was considered equivalent to that of the regular form of crucifixion, shows how immensely painful death on the cross could be.

There were variations in how crucifixions were conducted. In some cases, the victim's arms would be secured with rope, while, less commonly, their palms or wrists would literally be nailed to the wood. Designs of crucifixes also differed, and the traditional cross shape was far from standard. Early depictions of Jesus even have him crucified on a single pole with no cross-bar.

Sometimes, the victims would carry the cross beam to the place where they would be crucified. They would not carry the entire cross, as artistic depictions often show, because the assembly of the cross itself was carried out at the location of the crucifixion. The victim would be forced to lie down on the cross, to which they were then fixed, after which it would be hauled up into the air.

While the act of slowly dying from starvation and exposure is itself agonizing, additional tortures were frequently applied to the victims. They were usually stripped naked and insects would be naturally attracted to their bodies, but this process could be sped up by smearing honey on them. They could be stabbed, whipped, and any number of mutilations could be inflicted. Depending on their severity, these extra elements could be a blessing in disguise, as they would most likely hasten the death of the victims, whereas otherwise they could linger for days as their body slowly perished.

Crucifixion was the worst punishment for a citizen of Rome, as it was reserved for those of the lowest social standing, designed to humiliate and expose the dying victim to ridicule, forced to urinate and defecate in public. Mass crucifixions were sometimes intended to stigmatize an entire social group, such as rebels, and they presented a frightening spectacle. When the slave rebellion of Spartacus failed in 71 BC, approximately 6,000 of his followers were crucified along the Appian Way, which ran 320 miles between Capua and Rome.

However, as Roman society became Christianized, crucifixion took on the connotation that it has today, and the act itself was banned by Constantine the Great, the first Christian Roman emperor, in AD 337. While its abolition was an act of compassion, there was no shortage of similarly grim and humiliating public punishments available to replace it.

GLADIATORS

ABOVE: This mosaic from the third century depicts a gladiator killing a Christian, and is part of the floor of a palace in Curium, Cyprus.

Gladiatorial combat and the entertainments surrounding them were the primary form of mass entertainment in the early Roman empire. Gladiatorial games were often employed by political rivals to court popularity, and as a useful distraction in times of turmoil or civil unrest. No matter what else happened within the empire, from its conversion to Christianity to its eventual decline, its rulers always could depend on the popularity of the games to entertain and sometimes distract the masses. The games depicted a microcosm of Rome's own military conquests, with gladiators sometimes enacting the types of battles the inhabitants of Rome imagined going on in the corners of the empire, and sometimes even featuring some of those conquered foes, pressed into service in a version of their own defeat.

The majority of gladiators were taken from the lower ranks of Roman society: slaves captured in military conquests, convicted thieves and murderers, and rebels. These were another type of slave, just one with a more dangerous occupation and a strange form of celebrity if they were successful. The world of the gladiatorial games was filled with cruelty and a twisted sense of humor that often forced its participants into contests they had no chance of winning.

Combat was divided in various types, from gladiators fighting each other in a range of combinations: man on man; two versus one; in teams with different weapons to *venationes* (beast hunts) and *bestiarii* (beast fighting). Exotic animals from many different countries in the empire were brought out into the arenas, some for fights, others simply to be displayed if they were too valuable

DOCUMENTS

ITEMS 1 AND 2: TONAYUCA NOTEBOOK

A sketch from the Notebooks of Tonayuca in 1567. It depicts a Spaniard with a multiple-tailed whip lashing native prisoners in Mexico. Natives could receive disproportionate punishment for any transgression.

ITEM 3: CONSTITUTIO CRIMINALIS CAROLINA

Recognised as the first body of German criminal law, it was agreed in 1530 and ratified 2 years later. It established definitions and punishments for major crimes, notably witchcraft, for which it specified death by fire. It was also a basis for the use of obtaining confessions through torture. (For translation see overleaf).

ITEM 4: WALLACE SAFE CONDUCT PASS

A safe conduct pass for William Wallace from Philip IV of France, 33 November 1298. He had entered France to petition the king for help in Scotland's battle for independence. He later returned to Scotland, where he was subsequently caught and executed.

ITEM 3: CONSTITUTIO CRIMINALIS CAROLINA

Constitutio Criminalis Carolina

The penal code of His Serene Highness, the omnipotent and unconquerable Emperor Charles the Fifth, and the Holy Roman Empire/ upheld, compiled and enacted at the Diets of Augsburg and Regensburg / in the years [15]30 and 32.

By the grace and privilege of the Emperor

ae esta casa que al tiangues fue a dos vnos tributos a pedim^to de vn español el cual en ben
... de el arma / se pur que vn ... alguaziles con que ... los amenazo ... que ...
tar) y a vno dellos asio de los cabellos) con el ... le llamano / metio en ... y ...)
... de ... que ... de la ... en que la ... y el ... corregidor hizo lo que
... de ... -

q̃ un dia vino el dho fran^co mugarino

y m̃do a un hijo de Joseph Carmona pablo jacobo

y le m̃do que le midiese [illegible] e aver [illegible]

para dar a una crecençia del [illegible]

e porq̃ no lo quiso hazer le prendio [illegible]

e puso le en un cepo [illegible] el indio y que [illegible]

[illegible] de la carçel cayo malo y murio

a [illegible] que [illegible]

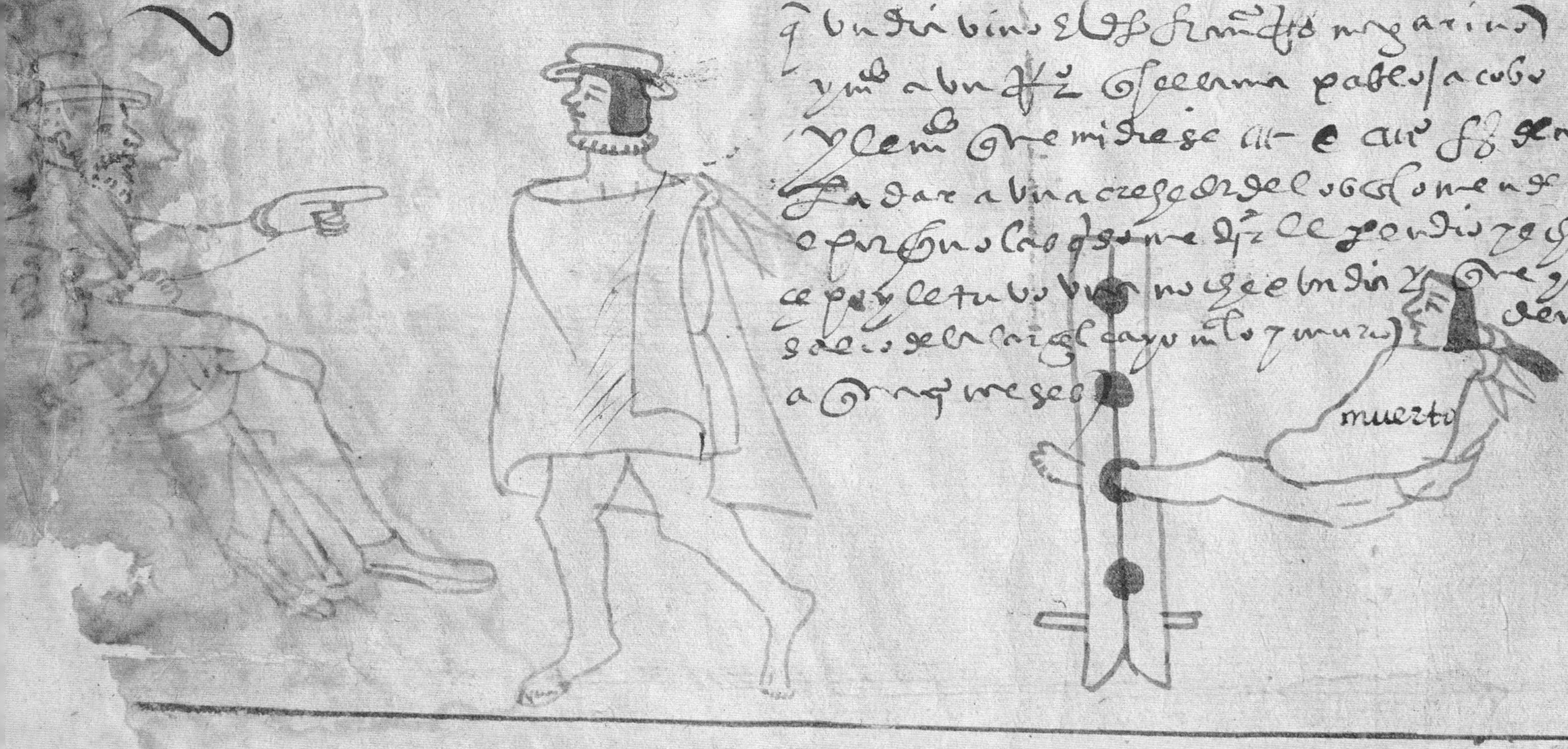

DEs allerdurchleuchtig=sten großmechtigstẽ vn=überwindtlichsten Key=ser Karls des fünfften: vnnd des heyligen Römischen Reichs peinlich gerichts ord=nung/auff den Reichsztägen zu Augspurgk vnd Regenspurgk/iñ jaren dreissig/vñ zwey vnd dreissig gehalten/auff=gericht vnd beschlossen.

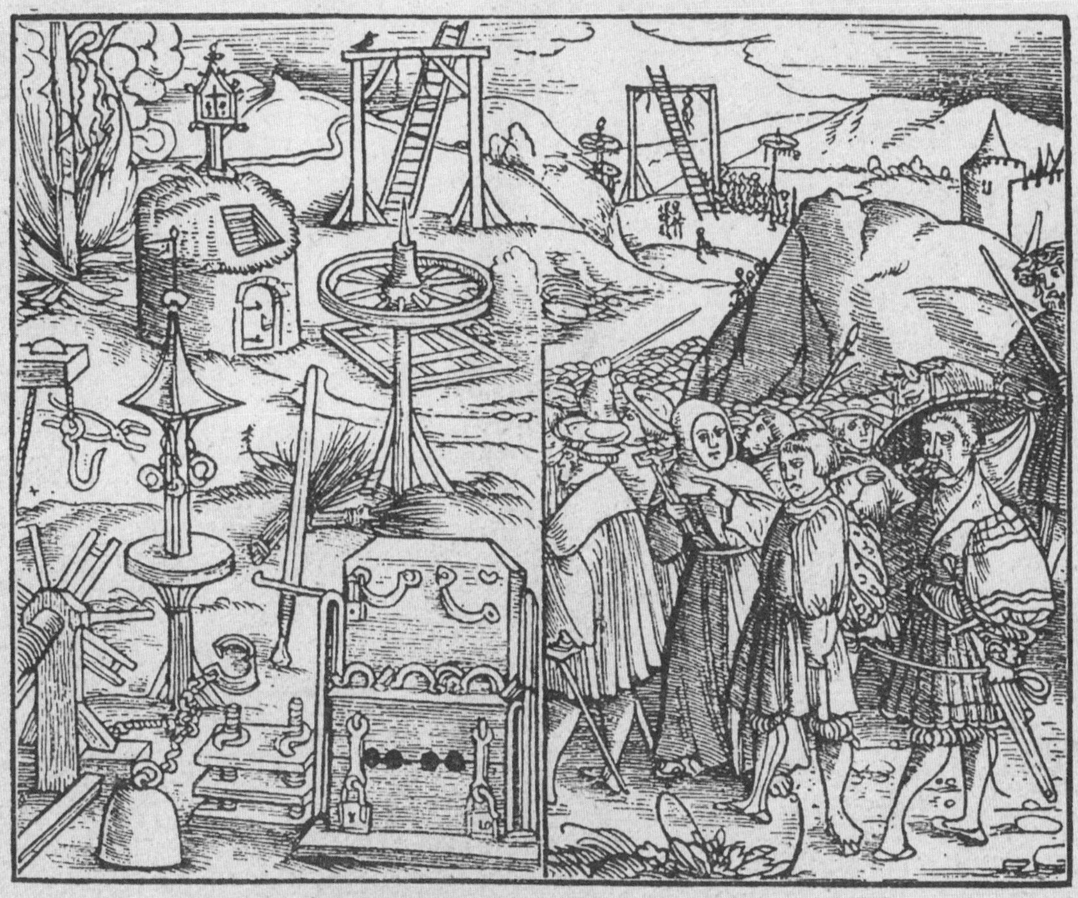

Cum gratia et priuilegio Imperiali.

Excell(enti) d(omi)ne et matri sue in xpo k(arissi)me, d(omi)ne Alienor(e) dei gr(aci)a regine
Anglie d(omi)ne Hib(er)nie et duc(isse) Aquitan(ie), soror [illegible] p(er)missio(n)e [illegible]
[illegible] abb(at)issa, (et) salute(m) (et) sp(irit)ualiu(m) orac(i)o(n)um suffrag(i)a devota. Confiteri
plen(itu)d(in)e(m) mortaliu(m) humana condic(i)o q(uam)q(ue) nos cordis [illegible]
et sanguine v(est)ro n(ost)ra posset religio decorari licet refferendo dolem(us) [illegible] sic
in eo cu(m) maior honor [illegible] regie maiestati et [illegible] ornamenta
decoris in capite ponit q(uam) in membris [illegible] d(omi)ne A. dei gr(aci)a
regin(e) Angl(ie) matris d(omi)ni regis [illegible] ipsam filiam [illegible]
ibid(em) [illegible] regiam maiestatem [illegible] successionib(us) [illegible]
ut p(ost) decessum [illegible] ab q(u)a ibid(em) [illegible]
[illegible] obtinere [illegible]
p(ri)mum [illegible] remedio [illegible] suis temporibus nos decorare
hoc a vob(is) [illegible] et nob(is) et conventui n(ost)ro filiab(us) v(est)ris [illegible]
sp(eci)al(iter) vob(is) [illegible] ex affectu
recomendam(us) [illegible] maiestas regal(is) [illegible]

to waste. Many animals like lions and tigers actually had to be trained to attack and kill human beings, having no natural instinct to do so.

The type of weapons and combat employed in encounters between gladiators were varied, from the net and trident-wielding *retiarii* to the *hoplomachus*, modeled on the hoplite warriors who had fought against the Roman conquest of Greece.

The gladiators who suffered the most were the *noxii*, those who were considered worthless owing to the nature of their crimes or transgressions. Their punishments were twisted, from pitting them weaponless against animals (the infamous "throwing Christians to the lions") to making them act out famous mythical deaths. They could be dressed up as animals and hunted or simply made to fight each other blindfolded with blunt weapons.

While those fated to die because of their pre-gladiatorial crimes were called *damnati*, those who were not condemned to death in the arena still had a very short lifespan. The only way to keep alive was to fight ferociously and well. Those who were defeated in the arena might be spared by the presiding magistrate if they were popular enough with the crowd, but those who were not were despatched with a killing blow to the neck. Some people had greater fighting instinct than others, and although larger slaves were often chosen to be gladiators, any Roman who felt their house slave was no longer useful could sell them into gladiatorial service. Although any injuries would be treated as well as possible after battles, some would inevitably be crippling. Being forced into battle after battle, with often unfair odds, whether you chose to or not, certainly qualifies as a form of torture. But gladiators could create a life for themselves, even marry and have children under some circumstances, as long as it was within the boundaries of their own circumscribed world. It is the *noxii* who were the true torture victims of these games, and their bodies did not even receive a decent burial. They were usually just dumped, sometimes in the river.

The Colosseum

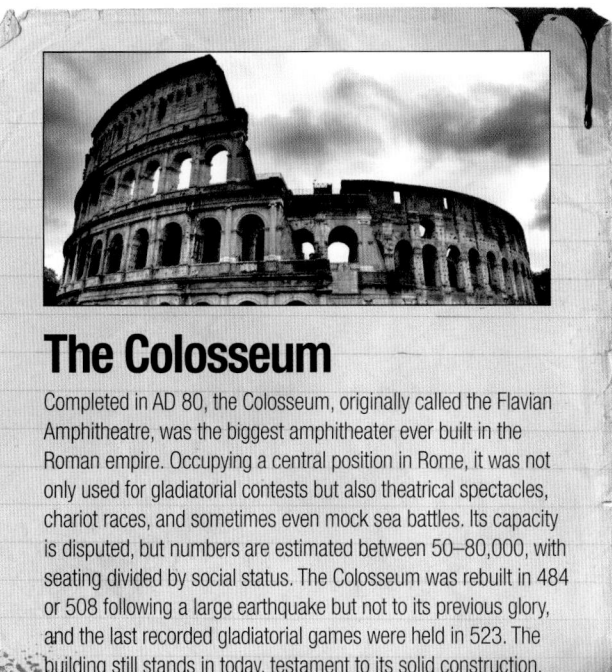

Completed in AD 80, the Colosseum, originally called the Flavian Amphitheatre, was the biggest amphitheater ever built in the Roman empire. Occupying a central position in Rome, it was not only used for gladiatorial contests but also theatrical spectacles, chariot races, and sometimes even mock sea battles. Its capacity is disputed, but numbers are estimated between 50–80,000, with seating divided by social status. The Colosseum was rebuilt in 484 or 508 following a large earthquake but not to its previous glory, and the last recorded gladiatorial games were held in 523. The building still stands in today, testament to its solid construction.

BELOW LEFT: Carved ivory reliefs depicting gladiators in combat with animals, while a Roman emperor watches. Man vs Bear, Bear vs Snake and Bear vs Bear are shown.

BELOW: A Christian martyr tied to a stake, about to be killed by lions in the Colosseum. This picture shows the victim with an almost beatific expression before her sacrifice.

TRIALS BY ORDEAL

Although much torture is motivated by sadism, or for the purposes of perverted entertainment, in the Middle Ages it still seemed like the best way to resolve issues of the guilt or innocence of those accused of crimes. Regular trials seemed to be dogged by people bearing false witness either for or against the accused.

The answer was to leave it up to God. Trials by ordeal were common in England until the twelfth century, when Henry II tried to suppress them (by the Assizes of Clarendon in 1166). They were tortuous, occasionally deadly, tests that the accused was subjected to. Sometimes innocence was proven if you survived a dangerous one, as God was seen as having saved you with a miracle, whereas at other times survival meant that you had somehow employed diabolical powers to avoid punishment and you would then be executed. Which view was preferred was inconsistent. The use of trial by ordeal goes back to ancient laws like the Babylonian Law Code of Hammurabi, and required absolute faith in the power of God to show his hand.

Trials by fire, a common ordeal, did not always involve the subject's being set on fire. Instead it was more common to have the victim walk barefoot over six, nine or even 12 red-hot ploughshares, sometimes blindfolded. The victim's feet would either be inspected at once or wrapped up and left for three days. If there was no sign of marks, then the victim was declared innocent as God had healed the wounds, but if not they would be sentenced and possibly executed.

ABOVE: St. Francis of Assisi walking through fire before the Sultan of Egypt and his scholars to prove his faith. Legend states he was not burned.

BELOW: A seventeenth-century woodcut depicting a suspected witch undergoing a trial by water in a ducking stool.

A legend suggested that in AD 1050, Emma of Normandy, who was suspected of infidelity with Aelfwine, the Bishop of Winchester, was sentenced to walk across hot ploughshares, but was so distracted and innocent she managed to do so without realizing. It seems unlikely that this was the case for the majority of those accused. Other trials by fire involved being made to hold a hot iron in the hand, or in the mouth, with the same subsequent inspection and conviction if burns were found.

Trials by water tended to involve rivers or lakes. A familiar torture device is the ducking stool, which lowered the victim into water where they could be held for a time. This is again something which has been portrayed comically, but the reality was a form of repeated drowning which led to the death of the occupant. Another trial was being cast into a river with a mill-stone tied round the neck. If the victim survived—clearly an unlikely occurrence—they were declared to be innocent.

Joan of Arc (1412–31)

Joan of Arc was born in 1412 to humble peasant origins, but became a commander of French forces during the Hundred Years' War, partly because she believed she had been contacted by God and told to drive the English out of France. Some claimed that her divine insights were in fact sent by the devil. She was sold to the English by the Burgundians, who captured her in 1430 and was then tried by a religious court. Found guilty, she was burned at the stake.

ABOVE: Queen Emma of Normandy, said to have been forced to walk across hot ploughshares.

Boiling water was also used for trials of ordeal. Victims had to put their hands into a pan full of it to retrieve a stone. This form of trial was first recorded as early as the sixth century AD, but was still in use 500 years later. Once again, if the victim's burns healed they were regarded to be innocent.

In trial by combat, the accused would simply fight the accuser. If the accused won, it would not be said to be through their skill, but rather because God had chosen the winner. This form of trial obviously favored skilled fighters, who were given *carte blanche* to accuse people of any number of crimes.

Another type of ordeal by combat was used for criminal soldiers. Called "running the gauntlet," the phrase was originally "running the gantelope." The victim was stripped to the waist, and had to run between two lines of his fellow soldiers who would beat him with cudgels, or other weaponry. If he survived, he was said to have been fated to do so, but survival for the hapless soldier, as

HANGING, DRAWING, AND QUARTERING

The extremely brutal and excessively elaborate nature of this torture was deliberate, as it was the ultimate sanction, reserved for those who committed what was at the time the worst crime possible: high treason. It was first recorded during the reign of Henry III in 1241. The Treason Act of 1351 sealed the punishment into law, as well as clarifying what constituted treason.

Each of its stages could be considered a horrific torture on its own. First, the victim would be taken to a public place. They were hanged, until they passed out at the brink of death. Then they would be revived, and disembowelled, usually after castration, but kept alive so that they could see their own organs being thrown onto a fire. They would not be allowed to die until their heart had been ripped out and shown to them. The victim would then be beheaded, and their body be cut into four pieces, each intended to be displayed in different parts of the kingdom as a warning. The victim's severed head would also be put on show, mounted on a pike in a public place.

It was very common for the remains of executed prisoners to be put on display. Just as the Romans would leave victims' bodies up on crucifixes or

BELOW: A manuscript showing Hugh Despenser the Younger being disembowelled on a ladder, with a fire at the bottom to burn his organs once they had been extracted.

broken on a wheel, so people in the Middle Ages would expose corpses in metal cages or mounted above city or castle gates, or along bridges, such as London Bridge. Death, and the horrific consequences of crime, were an ever-present reality for medieval people. But hanging, drawing, and quartering was the cruellest punishment possible.

The origin of the word "drawing" in this torture's name is disputed by historians. Some claim it is the pulling or "drawing" out of the entrails when the victim is eviscerated, whereas others maintain it refers to the victim being dragged to the place of their execution behind a horse and cart.

Although there were certain elements in hanging, drawing, and quartering that never changed, others could be altered from time to time. For example, Hugh Despenser the Younger, an English knight, arch-manipulator of court intrigues and favorite of Edward II, was sentenced to be executed in this manner in 1326, after he was removed from power by Queen Isabella and her forces in a royal coup and declared a traitor. He was dragged through the streets behind a cart with four horses, taunted by baying crowds all the way. This public humiliation was also a form of torture in itself, though one usually reserved for unfaithful wives.

While hanging, drawing, and quartering was a special punishment, its use was not infrequent in the medieval period. The endless series of shifting allegiances, coups and counter-coups, and secret conspiracies that marked the period meant that one minute you could be a stalwart member of the Royal Household, and the next a disgusting traitor. Sometimes, the punishment was even inflicted on entire groups of people, such as those involved in the Babington plot of 1586 that led to the death of Mary Queen of Scots. In 1605 all the Gunpowder Plot conspirators led by Guy Fawkes (see page 31) were sentenced to be hung, drawn, and quartered. In 1685, a group of judges led by Lord Chief Justice Jeffreys sentenced almost 1,000 rebels to death, and at least 300 of them were hung, drawn, and quartered in an event known as the Bloody Assizes.

BELOW LEFT: The execution of William Wallace.

BELOW: The events of the Bloody Assizes depicted on playing cards.

William Wallace (died 1305)

Sir William Wallace was a Scottish landowner who, in a reaction against the English takeover of Scottish rule in 1292, led armies against the far superior forces of King Edward I (nicknamed Longshanks). After a series of surprisingly successful battles against the English, Wallace was captured and turned over to them by Ralph Rae, a fellow Scotsman. He was tried in a biased court and sentenced to be hung, drawn, and quartered. After the execution, his head was preserved with tar and mounted on London Bridge.

INQUISITIONS

Inquisitions, official bodies organized to investigate religious heresy and deviance from orthodox beliefs, emerged out of the religious paranoia and turmoil of their originating countries. Each of the Inquisitions was in fact a tool of political suppression and control, as well as unleashing massive waves of persecution, which on occasion bordered on genocide. The Inquisitions all had in common a belief in the holy power of torture as a way to extract the confession of a perceived truth out of people, and even somehow to save their souls.

Every religious culture has its own history of persecutions and trials, but the term Inquisition is generally only applied to those conducted under the aegis of the Roman Catholic Church. While there were previous outbreaks of religious fervor, leading to executions and pogroms, the earliest recognized Inquisition began in 1184. The Episcopal Inquisition, as it was called at the time, was a response to a growing number of offshoot Christian sects and cults that dared to interpret the word of God in their own way, such as the Cathars of the Languedoc area of southern France. It was considered necessary to establish who had transgressed and to demonstrate how unacceptable this was. The inquisitors would travel from town to town and, although they frequently used trials by ordeal, they would also question whether the accuser had any kind of grievance against the accused, because they wanted to avoid being misled

RIGHT: A portrait of Pope Innocent IV. In 1252 he issued the Papal Bull *Ad extirpanda* which authorized the use of torture during the Inquisition.

BELOW: A large *auto de fé*, with a crowd of citizens gathered to witness the supposedly guilty people being burned at the stake.

ABOVE: A group of prisoners await either punishment or execution by the Inquisition in this scene painted by Lucas Y Padilla in 1851.

Tomás de Torquemada (1420–1498)

Torquemada was the first Grand Inquisitor of Spain, a former Dominican monk elevated to the position by the king and queen in 1483 because of his position as their advisor. He took to his job with gusto, authorizing the expulsion of Jews, the burning of non-Catholic books, and the persecution of anyone who dared to criticize the Inquisition. While not necessarily any more fanatical than other inquisitors, he was the public face of the Inquisition, and a target of incredible hatred, long after his death in 1498 of old age.

LEFT: Tomás de Torquemada with King Ferdinand II and Queen Isabella in 1478.

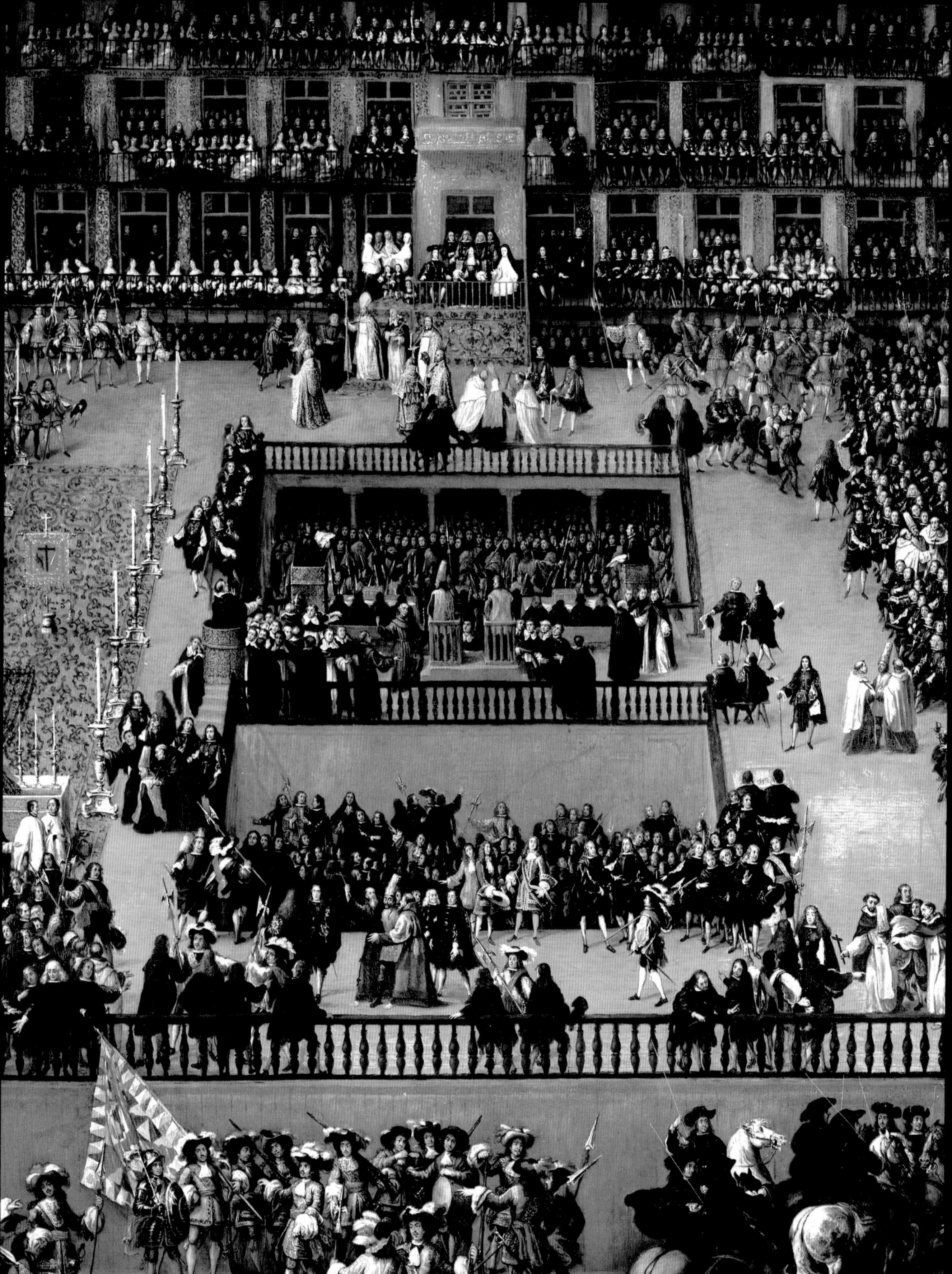

by those harboring grudges. Nevertheless, miscarriages of justice were likely as torture was authorized, though confession under torture alone was not at this point considered valid. The Inquisition employed almost all the tortures this book has already looked at and many of those yet to be described, its torturers released from all ideas of mercy save what their own religious fervor demanded.

The Spanish Inquisition was the most famous of all, created in 1478 as a holy tribunal by the reigning Spanish monarchs Ferdinand II and Isabella I. Whereas the medieval Inquisition was controlled by the pope, theirs was intended to be entirely their own tool, as an aid to establishing their authority in their newly united kingdom and over the Muslim emirate of Granada after its conquest in 1492.

They began by expelling all Jews from their kingdom, and persecuting the *conversos*, those said to have converted to Christianity from Judaism, but who were still suspected of practicing in secret. Later attention fell on Moriscos, who had converted to Catholicism from Islam, and anyone else thought to have transgressed, through sodomy, witchcraft, or other acts seen as threatening orthodoxy. However, these were easy labels that could be applied to anybody whom the authorities decided to victimize.

There would be public displays of those who were considered guilty, known as an *auto de fé* or "act of faith." The sentences would be read and then the condemned would be executed, usually by burning at the stake. Crowds would howl with approval, although for obvious reasons showing any disapproval of the proceedings may itself have attracted the unwelcome attentions of the inquisitors.

The Portuguese Inquisition was formally created in 1536 and closely followed the model of its Spanish counterpart, although its main target was to expel those Jews that had left Spain. It later expanded its operations into Portuguese colonies as well, such as Goa (in India) and Brazil.

A similar outflowing of religious fervor led to the Roman Inquisition, established in 1542, as a way for the pope to exercise the same level of control over his home city as he enjoyed elsewhere.

Whether or not those involved in the Inquisitions truly held the strong religious convictions they required from their victims is a matter of speculation. Many no doubt simply acted out of self-preservation, while the sheer inventiveness of the unpleasant tortures they inflicted definitely points to a high level of sadism. Over time, the Inquisitions simply faded and lost power to other, more secular institutions.

OPPOSITE: An 1683 painting by Francisco Rizi depciting an *auto de fé* being peformed on Plaza Mayor in Madrid.

RIGHT: Two heretics are burned as St. Dominic of Guzman watches. It is unclear if he was involved in the Inquisition.

STRAPPADO

Strappado, also known as squassation or the torture of the pulley, was one of the favored tortures of the various Inquisitions, but has been popular among many cultures throughout history.

The victim had their hands tied behind their back, and then a rope would be wound through a pulley or similar device, and hoisted up off the ground so that they were suspended by a single cord. In this position, the muscles and bones of the arms were stretched backward dangerously and very painfully, and ultimately every part of the body put under incredible strain.

This torture has a few qualities in common with crucifixion, in particular the type of pain it caused and, if left long enough, the manner of death. While strappado was more likely to be practiced indoors, in a torture chamber, victims were sometimes strung up and left to die this way in public.

To increase the level of pain inflicted, it was common to attach iron weights to the victim's body and legs, sometimes up to 100 pounds, causing even further strain on the muscular and skeletal structure.

If by this point the victim had not confessed, or had in any other way dissatisfied the torturer, they could then be hauled by the pulley much higher into the air, sometimes up to twice the victim's height, and then suddenly dropped back down again, shaking and traumatizing every part of their body, dislocating limbs, and most likely causing permanent muscle and nerve damage. The fact that the victim could be hauled up and suspended, not knowing at what point they would be dropped, added an extra psychological element to the torture. Obviously, just as with crucifixion, other tortures could also be applied while the victim was on the strappado, from whipping to mutilation, and solid weaponry could be used to break bones.

Strappado's appeal to torturers in part lay in its simplicity. Other tortures required the presence of specialist equipment, the building of fires, or the assembly of large wooden or metal devices. Although a winch of sorts was

Niccolò Machiavelli (1469–1527)

Machiavelli was a writer and philosopher in Renaissance-era Italy, as well as a significant figure in the politics of the time. His most famous writing was *The Prince*, which espoused, possibly ironically, the philosophy of the end justifying the means. However, before he wrote this, he was responsible for the militia in Florence, and after the Medici took control of the area was accused of conspiracy and tortured by strappado. He did not confess and was eventually released.

LEFT: Torturers perform strappado on a condemned man. This is a fancifully complex mechanism for what is essentially a simple process.

required for strappado, at its most basic, all that was ultimately needed was a rope and a sturdy limb. The torture could even be conducted spontaneously, as with some mob-led lynchings.

Girolamo Savonarola, the Dominican friar and leader of the separatist state of Florence after the overthrow of the Medicis in 1494, led a huge inquisition-like purge on the society he oversaw, demanding a new stricter religious orthodoxy and railing against what he saw as needless excess and depravity. He initiated what was called the "Bonfire of the Vanities," in which assistants went to people's houses to take items considered morally dubious, such as paintings, ornaments, and literature, which would then be burned in a huge fire in Florence's largest piazza. However, after he fell out of favor in 1497, he was excommunicated and captured by a large mob, and fell into the hands of the Roman Inquisition. Accused of heresy and other crimes, he and his compatriots were extensively tortured in many ways, one of which was strappado. Once again, those who had at first wielded the instruments of torture had fallen prey to its clutches themselves.

Strappado continued to be popular long beyond the time of the Inquisition, as a horrifyingly effective but easy-to-construct torture device, and it is still used in some parts of the world by the police or the army. The human passion for sadism continues unabated.

ABOVE: A victim is hauled to an incredible height during a series of public executions. The drop from here would be instantly fatal.

BELOW: One man endures strappado, while around him others undergo a variety of similarly unpleasant tortures in a basement dungeon.

BREAKING

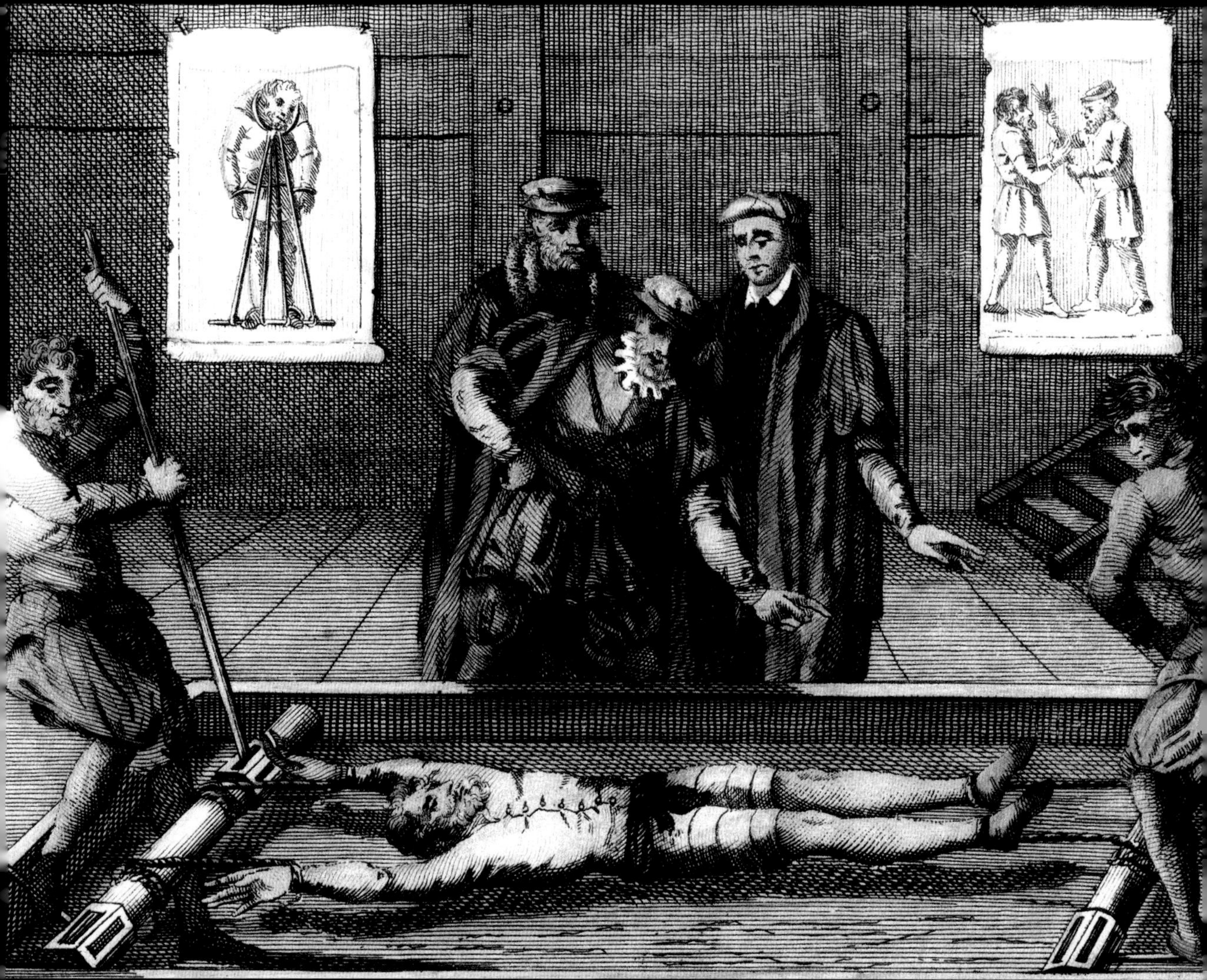

Tortures are often selected not just for the pain and suffering they cause, but also for the sense of anticipation and fear they instill in their victims. The rack is one of the best-known and frequently depicted torture instruments, in large part because of its popularity with the Spanish Inquisition (see pages 24–27). It may also be because its impact is seen as somehow comical, the person on the rack becoming elongated without any real ill effect. However, the reality of the rack is much more horrifying.

The victim would be secured on a long wooden frame with their hands and feet fastened at either end to a winding mechanism that, once turned, pulled in both directions, stretching the limbs beyond the limits of endurance. Ligaments popped and the muscles and skeletal structure tore, in some cases becoming permanently damaged, causing paralysis and muscular disorders as the victim's body lost its ability to flex and maintain coherence.

Where the rack differs from the strappado is that the level to which the

ABOVE: An English Protestant is tortured on the rack during the reign of Queen Mary. Cuthbert Sympson was also put in the Scavenger's Daughter (see page 35) and had an arrow thrust through his hand.

the agony. The idea was that the sense of control that the torturer exercises over the pain would increase the victim's sense of the Inquisitor's "god-given" power over life and death.

This drawing out of pain had another benefit to the Inquisition: people who were to be tortured in the same way could witness the slow destruction of those who came before them and, as a result, often chose to confess without the need for the torture to be inflicted on them.

The rack was also used in England, where it was frequently employed in the Tower of London. The ultimate intention of this torture was not necessarily the permanent crippling of the victim, and some of those subjected to the rack survived, but that does not diminish how horrifying the

Similar to the rack, but frequently put to a different purpose, was the breaking wheel. This was usually a man-sized wooden wheel, like that of a wagon, either placed on the ground or mounted on a series of poles. The victim was lashed to it with ropes, and their limbs stretched to their limit across its surface. Then the limbs would be broken, sometimes by smashing them with an iron hammer or a similarly heavy object. The victim's head would be smashed too, but the order in which this was conducted depended on the nature of the crime, with more severe crimes dictating that the neck be broken last.

Unlike the rack, breaking wheels were usually employed in the open air, at displays of the condemned, or at trials of heretics. After their death, the victim's body would be left on display, thereby mirroring other tortures such as crucifixion or hanging, drawing, and quartering (see pages 16–17). As with those forms of execution, other tortures could be inflicted either before or during the breaking of the limbs. However, as with crucifixion (see pages 22–23), some injuries could be considered merciful, since they would hasten the victim's death with a *coup de grâce* or "blow of mercy."

The person most strongly associated with the wheel was St. Catherine of Alexandria, hence its alternative name, the Catherine wheel. She lived in the early fourth century AD, and after becoming a Christian, proceeded to proselytize others, converting many, until the Roman emperor of the time ordered her captured and tortured on the wheel. Legend claims that when she touched the wheel it broke, and so she had to be beheaded instead. It is interesting that the wheel's most famous victim is claimed to have not actually been put on it.

ABOVE: A woodcut of several men being broken on the wheel during medieval times. When smashed their limbs would sometimes be twisted into normally impossible shapes.

BELOW: The execution of Robert Catesby, Guy Fawkes, and Thomas Percy in London.

Guy Fawkes (1570–1606)

Living in England in the seventeenth century, Guy Fawkes entered into a Catholic conspiracy to assassinate King James I (a Protestant) and kill a large number of other powerful figures by detonating a huge stock of gunpowder beneath the Houses of Parliament. It was his task to light the cache. Owing to a tip-off, he was captured and tortured for the names of his co-conspirators. It is unknown if the rack was actually used on him, but it was authorized and extremely likely to have been employed in his interrogation, although he eventually died by hanging.

CUTTING AND SAWING

Many tortures involve incisions, whether as an additional way of causing pain to supplement another torture, or as a prelude to flaying off the skin. However, the act of cutting can be itself a form of torture, without any other techniques involved.

Cutting is performed simply by using knives or other sharp implements such as saws to remove body parts piece by piece. This is a form of mutilation, but whereas the principle of an eye-for-an-eye would mean the perpetrator's crime would dictate what body parts were removed, here everything would be amputated, no matter what the crime. It is not hard to imagine how incredibly painful and traumatic this process would be, especially as the victim would be shown the various parts as they were removed.

Blood loss would clearly accelerate the victim's death, so experienced torturers would staunch and bandage the victim as they proceeded, to extend the agony for as long as possible. Alternatively, the wounds might be cauterized with a hot iron, which would itself cause extreme pain.

During the process, body parts could also be manipulated to cause extra pain; for example the throat might be cut and the tongue pulled through the wound, a torture that later became known as the Colombian neck-tie for its punitive use by drug cartels in the twentieth century.

As with many other tortures, this form of cutting would also render the individual's body unsuitable for display or for normal burial. Some cultures even believed that mutilations like this would persist through to the afterlife, rendering the individual essentially cursed forever.

Sawing was a similar type of torture, in which the body was divided into halves or quarters while the victim was still alive. This was a popular torture for public displays, almost like a grim version of the classic magic trick.

The victim would be hung between two poles, usually upside down. Then, a huge saw would be taken and the victim would be slowly cut in half, starting at the groin and working directly downward. They would remain conscious throughout most of this as the head and brain would naturally be reached last, and they would likely feel the sensation of their innards falling out and obeying the laws of gravity, flopping past their torso. This is not a torture where the victim had any chance of surviving, and so was used as a deterrent in a similar manner to hanging, drawing, and quartering (see pages 22–23).

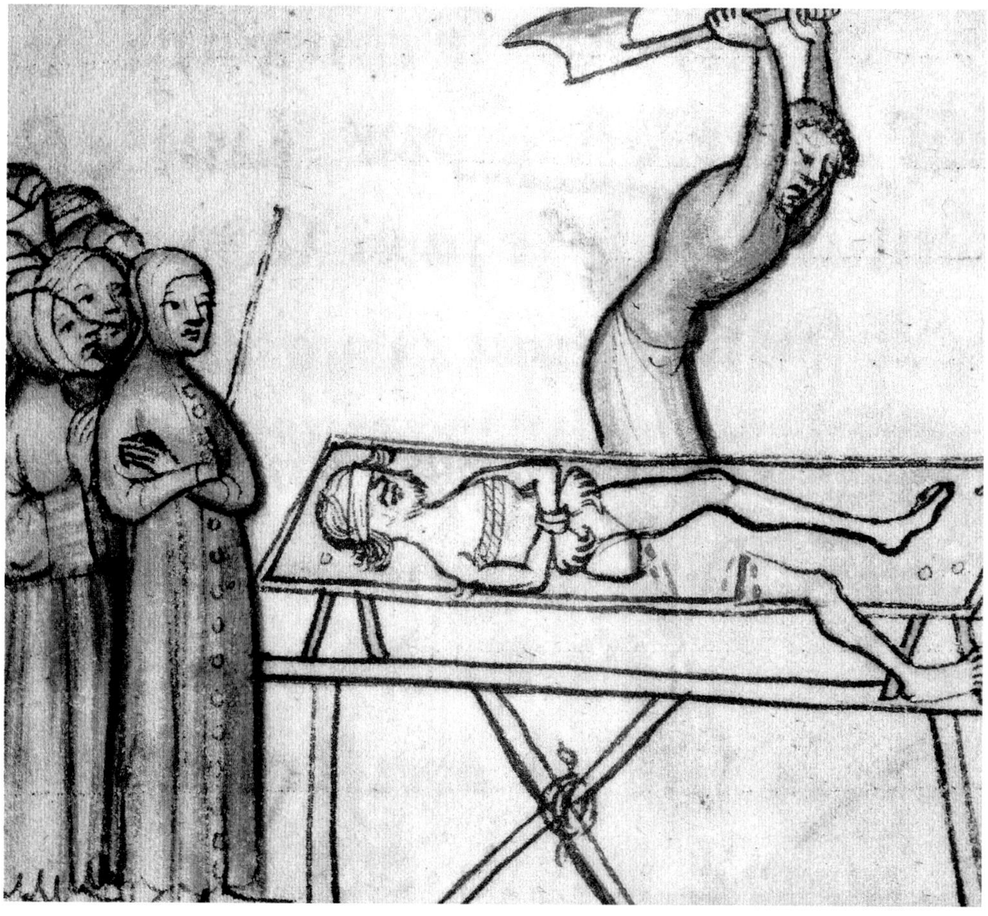

ABOVE: Bust of Emperor Caligula, notorious in legend for condemning both guilty and innocent to brutal punishments on a whim, particularly beheading and castration.

RIGHT: The torture and execution of Symon Poulliet in fourteenth-century France. He was tied down and his limbs were cut off with an axe, one after the other.

DOCUMENTS

ITEM 5: COMPILATION OF INSTRUCTIONS

Title page of Compilacion de las Instructiones del Officio de la Sancta Inquisition by Tomas de Torquemada. This book of rules and teachings for the Inquisition was published in 1576. (For translation see overleaf).

ITEM 6: GUY FAWKES' SIGNED CONFESSION

Guy Fawkes' confession, extracted under torture in 1606. Signed by Guido Fawkes and his torturers Sir John Popham, Sir Edward Coke & Mr. W. Wood (a clerk).

ITEM 7: POPE INNOCENT IV AUTHORIZATION OF TORTURE

A Papal Bull issued by Pope Innocent IV in 1250, authorising torture. The document includes a pen drawing of a heretic being burned at the stake.

ITEM 8: VILLON POEM

Text of "The Epitaph" by François Villon, also called "Balade of the Hanged." He was a French poet known for both frequenting and recording the criminal underworld of the time. He was subjected to water torture in 1462 due to a brawl amongst his friends at which he was ironically not present. (For translation see overleaf).

ITEM 5: COMPILATION OF INSTRUCTIONS

COMPILATION of the Instructions of the Office of the Holy Inquisition laid down by the Most Reverend Gentleman and Brother, Thomas de Torquemada, Prior of the monastery of the Holy Cross, Segovia, first Inquisitor General of the kingdoms and dominions of Spain; and by the other most reverend gentlemen inquisitors general who later succeeded, with regard to the rules to be observed in the exercise of the Holy Office and in which, on the one part, are set out in succession all instructions relating to the Inquisitors, and on the other part, those relating to each one of the officials and ministers of the Holy Office. These have been compiled in the manner ordered by the Most Illustrious and Most Reverend Gentleman Don Alonso Manrique, Cardinal of the Church of the Twelve Apostles, Archbishop of Seville, Inquisitor General of Spain.

ITEM 8: VILLON POEM

The Epitah by Francois Villon, translated by Algernon Charles Swinburne

Men, brother men, that after us yet live,
    Let not your hearts too hard against us be;
For if some pity of us poor men ye give,
    The sooner God shall take of you pity.
    Here are we five or six strung up, you see,
And here the flesh that all too well we fed
Bit by bit eaten and rotten, rent and shred,
    And we the bones grow dust and ash withal;
Let no man laugh at us discomforted,
    But pray to God that he forgive us all.

If we call on you, brothers, to forgive,
    Ye should not hold our prayer in scorn, though we
Were slain by law; ye know that all alive
    Have not wit alway to walk righteously;
    Make therefore intercession heartily
With him that of a virgin's womb was bred,
That his grace be not as a dry well-head
    For us, nor let hell's thunder on us fall;
We are dead, let no man harry or vex us dead,
    But pray to God that he forgive us all.

The rain has washed and laundered us all five,
    And the sun dried and blackened; yea, perdie,
Ravens and pies with beaks that rend and rive
    Have dug our eyes out, and plucked off for fee
    Our beards and eyebrows; never are we free,
Not once, to rest; but here and there still sped,
Drive at its wild will by the wind's change led,
    More pecked of birds than fruits on garden-wall;
Men, for God's love, let no gibe here be said,
    But pray to God that he forgive us all.

Prince Jesus, that of all art lord and head,
Keep us, that hell be not our bitter bed;
    We have nought to do in such a master's hall.
Be not ye therefore of our fellowhead,
    But pray to God that he forgive us all.

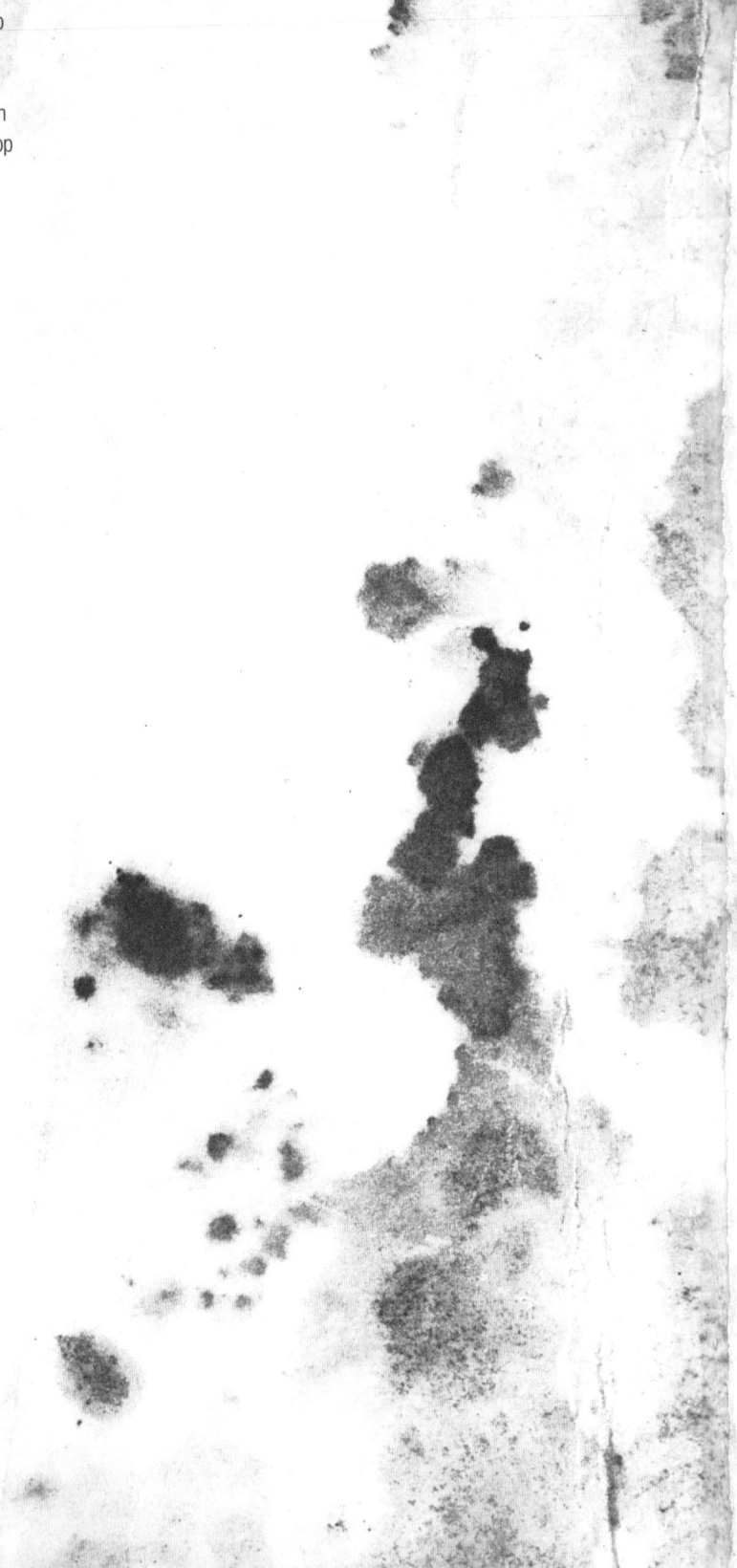

COPILACION

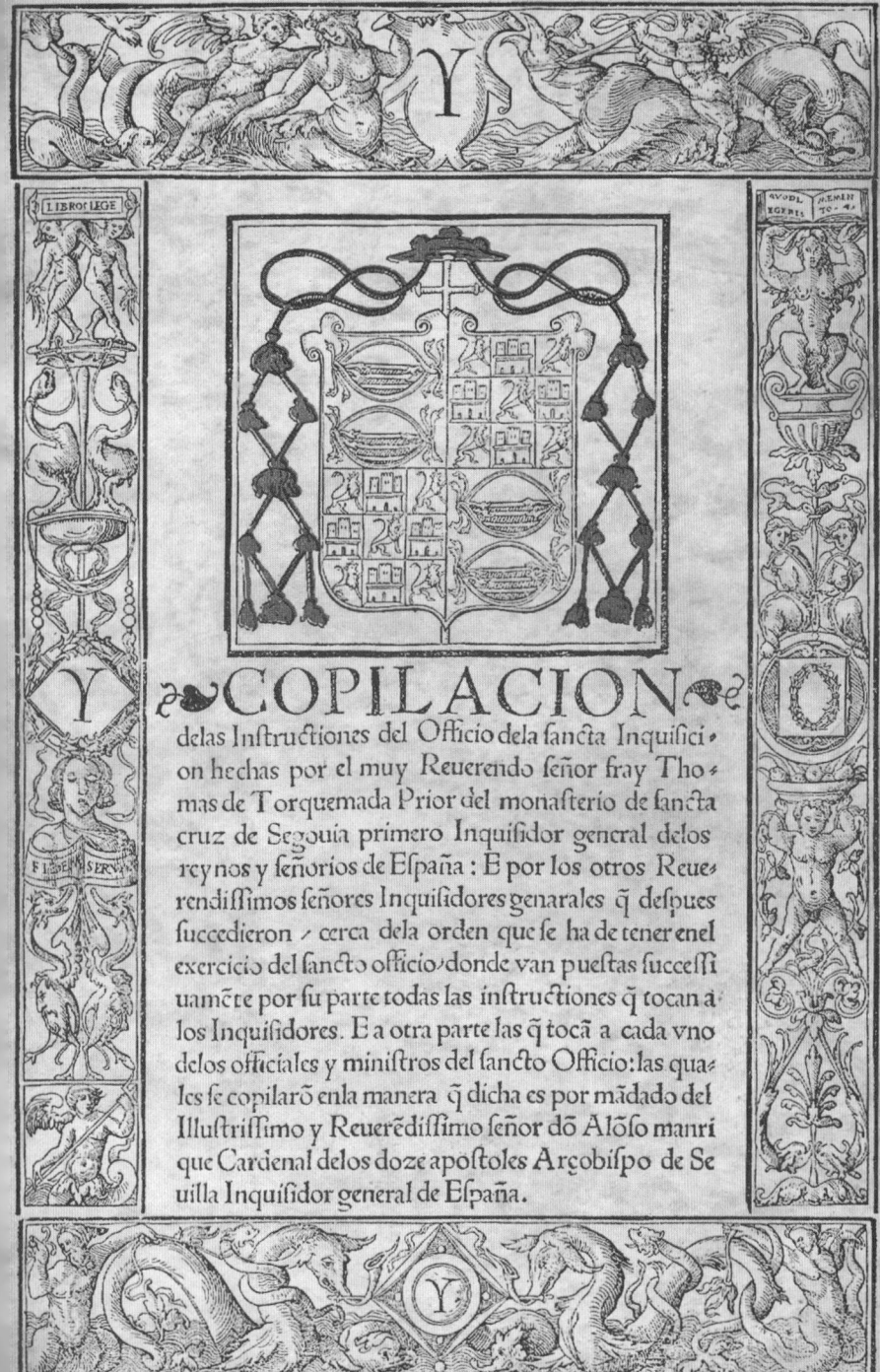

delas Inſtructiones del Officio dela ſancta Inquiſicion hechas por el muy Reuerendo ſeñor fray Thomas de Torquemada Prior del monaſterio de ſancta cruz de Segouia primero Inquiſidor general delos reynos y ſeñorios de Eſpaña: E por los otros Reuerendiſſimos ſeñores Inquiſidores genarales q̃ deſpues ſuccedieron, cerca dela orden que ſe ha de tener enel exercicio del ſancto officio, donde van pueſtas ſucceſſiuamẽte por ſu parte todas las inſtructiones q̃ tocan a los Inquiſidores. E a otra parte las q̃ tocã a cada vno delos officiales y miniſtros del ſancto Officio: las quales ſe copilarõ enla manera q̃ dicha es por mãdado del Illuſtriſſimo y Reuerẽdiſſimo ſeñor dõ Alõſo manrique Cardenal delos doze apoſtoles Arçobiſpo de Seuilla Inquiſidor general de Eſpaña.

The declaration of Guido Fawke
taken the 9 of Nov 1605

He confesseth that Mr Catesby told this exam[inant]
that Sir Edw Baynham was directed by
them to go to the Pope and to acquaint
him with the state of the Catholiques
of England: and that Sir Edw Baynham
[illegible] [illegible] [illegible] [illegible]
might have [illegible], and the Pope's [illegible]
for the relief of Catholiques after the
blowe of the powder had taken effect
and that the first [illegible] might have
been made of Sir Edw Baynham to the
Pope as should have been thought
fitte.

Guido Fawkes

[illegible]

J. Popham

Edw: Coke

W Waad

J: 425. n° 1 --

n° 410

Hec est forma secundum quam debet im-
perator terra aptica ḡᵒ hereticos.

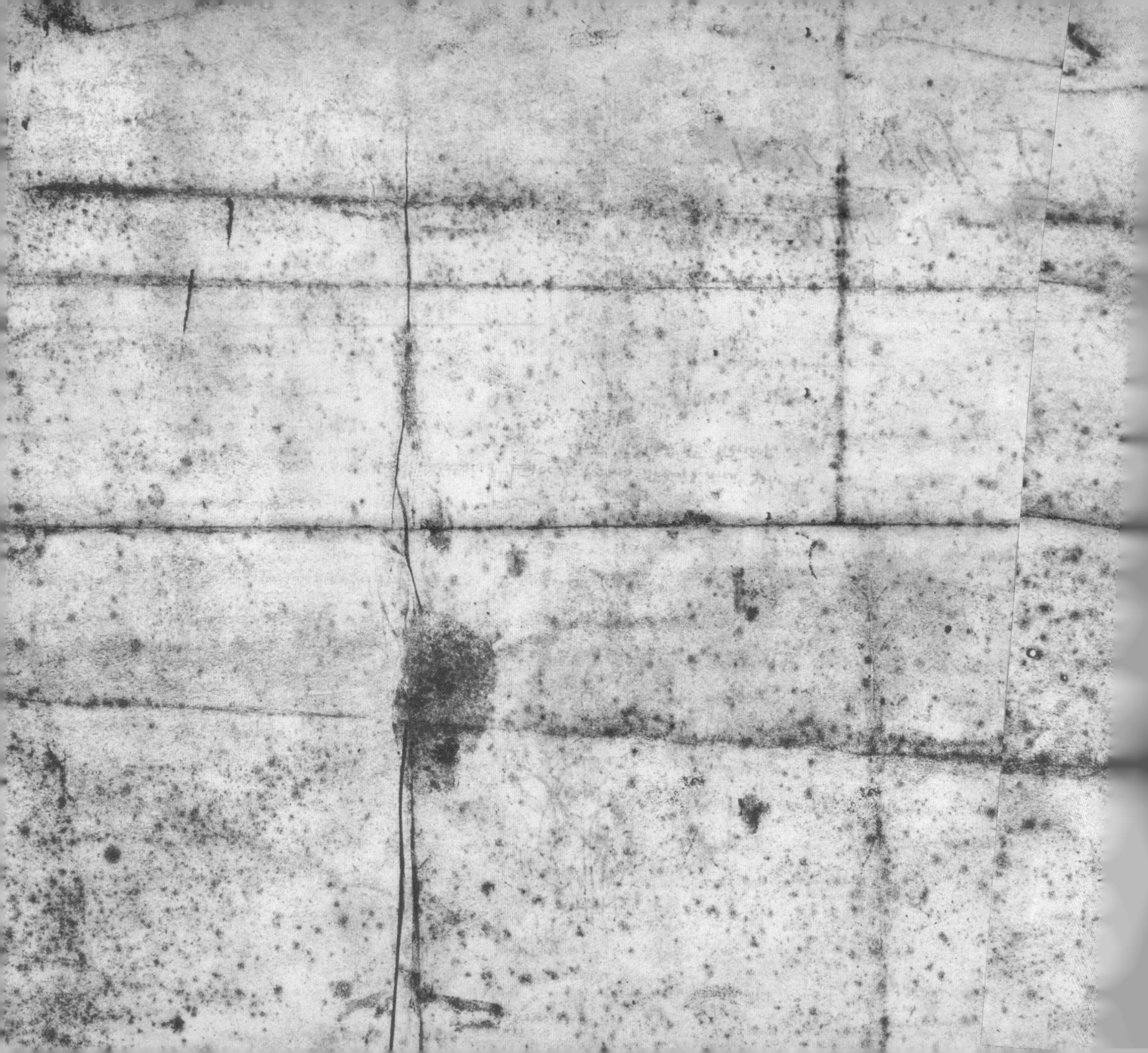

Epitaphe Villon

Freres humains qui apres nous vivez
Nayez les cueurs contre nous endurcis
Car se pitie de nous povres avez
Dieu en aura plus tost de vous mercis
Vous nous voyez cy attachez cinq six
Quant de la chair que trop avons nourrie
Elle est pieca devoree et pourrie
Et nous les os devenons cendre et pouldre
De nostre mal personne ne sen rie
Mais priez dieu que tous nous vueille absouldre

Se freres vous clamons pas nen devez
Avoir desdaing quoy que fusmes occis
Par justice toutesfois vous savez
Que tous hommes nont pas bon sens rassis
Excusez nous puis que sommes transsis
Envers le filz de la vierge marie
Que sa grace ne soit pour nous tarie
Nous preservant de linfernal fouldre
Nous sommes mors ame ne nous harie
Mais priez dieu etc.

La pluye nous a buez et lavez
Et le soleil dessechez et noirciz
Pyes et corbeaulx nous ont les yeulx cavez
Et arrache la barbe et les sourcilz
Jamais nul temps nous ne sommes assis
Puis ca puis la comme le vent varie
A son plaisir sans cesser nous charie
Plus becquetez doyseaulx que dez a couldre
Ne soiez donc de nostre confrarie
Mais priez dieu

Prince Jhesus qui sur tous a maistrie
Garde quenfer nait de nous seigneurie
A luy nayons que faire ne que souldre
Humains icy na point de mocquerie
Mais priez dieu etc.

Pendulum

In this uncommon form of torture, the victim would be strapped down and a huge metal pendulum swung above them, with a sharp blade affixed to the end. As it swung, it would slowly lower, bringing the blade ever closer to slicing into the victim. The intent was to drive the victim to a level of fear and anticipation that would almost lead them to becoming deranged. It is for this reason that Edgar Allan Poe featured one in his story *The Pit and the Pendulum.*

RIGHT: An illustration produced for Poe's famous story.

In some circumstances, a victim could be sawn in half using a piece of rope. This was accomplished by using a rope composed of particularly hard fibers, pulled down at the ends with iron weights, and manipulated back and forth until it ripped its way through the victim's body. This would be potentially even more painful than sawing with a blade, as the bluntness of the rope, the feeling of the fibers, and the increased time and effort involved would cause excruciating suffering.

A strange sideline of these particular tortures, and their popularity as a form of entertainment, was a curiosity about the make-up of the human body. Anatomy was not hugely advanced at the time these tortures were in use, and seeing the components of the human body displayed so brazenly, and methodically, must have been a powerful draw. As people came to understand more about the body and how it functioned, this curiosity may have abated, but the increased knowledge in itself would ultimately lead to ever more creative forms of torture and coercion.

BELOW: Persian art depicting a victim being sawn in half from the top of the skull. The executioners use a curved two handed saw seemingly designed for the purpose.

CRUSHING

Fears of small, suffocating spaces, which can sometimes be magnified to the level of claustrophobia, are common in human culture, possibly because of the understandable threat of being trapped by a predator or buried alive in a landslide. While some tortures can involve the victim being shut into a small space and simply left there, the ones detailed here concentrated on the very specific act of being physically crushed by heavy weights or through immense pressure.

The most popular form of crushing torture was pressing, also known as *peine forte et dure* or "a strong and forceful punishment." It was most frequently used in England (and France) in the Middle Ages. The usual practice was to place the victim under a large board or door and then to apply heavy weights, one after the other, on top. Rocks or actual metal weights designed for the role might be used, depending on the purpose or spontaneity of the punishment. In some cases, no board was used at all and the weights were simply placed directly onto the individual, who would be tied down to prevent movement. Inevitably, after a certain weight was reached, bones would begin to break, muscle tissue to bruise and organs would be distorted, and eventually crushed. It was no doubt an agonizing death, and would be carried out in public. While common in Europe, pressing enjoyed limited popularity in America and only one man has ever been recorded dying that way—Giles Corey who suffered death by pressing in September 1692 after refusing to enter a plea when accused of witchcraft during the Salem witch trials.

Other cultures practiced similar techniques in different ways. In India, captive enemies were crushed by an elephant. As comical as this may sound to contemporary ears, it was a deadly serious practice. The victim would often be tied with ropes behind their back, then forced to lie or kneel on a rock or piece of wood, where the elephant would bear down upon them with its foot and tusks, either ending the victim's life quickly or, if it had been trained to prolong the pain, agonizingly slowly. Some elephants were so well trained that they could actually tear people limb from limb using their trunk.

If the torturer did not want to crush the entire victim, there was a wide variety of different devices designed for the crushing of individual body parts. In the head crusher, the entire skull was fitted between two metal plates, restrained at the neck, and then a threaded handle was turned, compressing the two together, crushing the jaw and skull, and causing the eyeballs to pop out of their sockets.

ABOVE LEFT: A captive undergoes crushing, one of many examples from historical records.

LEFT: The witchcraft trial of Giles Corey in Salem, Massachusetts, in 1692. He was sentenced to death by pressing

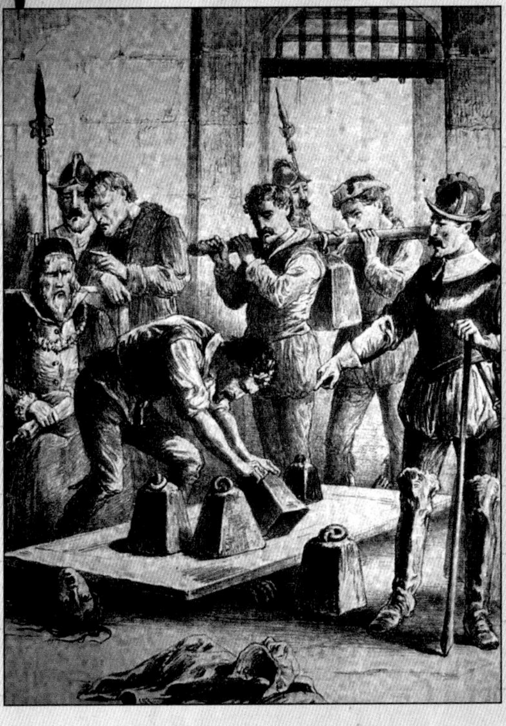

ABOVE: Margaret Clitherow being pressed to death.

St. Margaret Clitherow

Born into a prominent York family, Margaret Clitherow was an ordinary housewife until her conversion to Roman Catholicism, a religion facing persecution at the time from the Protestant establishment under Elizabeth I. She helped conduct secret Masses and harbored priests. Once caught, she was sentenced to being pressed after refusing to plead. She was laid on a large sharp-edged rock, a door was placed on top of her, and a huge number of weights placed on top of it until she died. She was canonized in 1970.

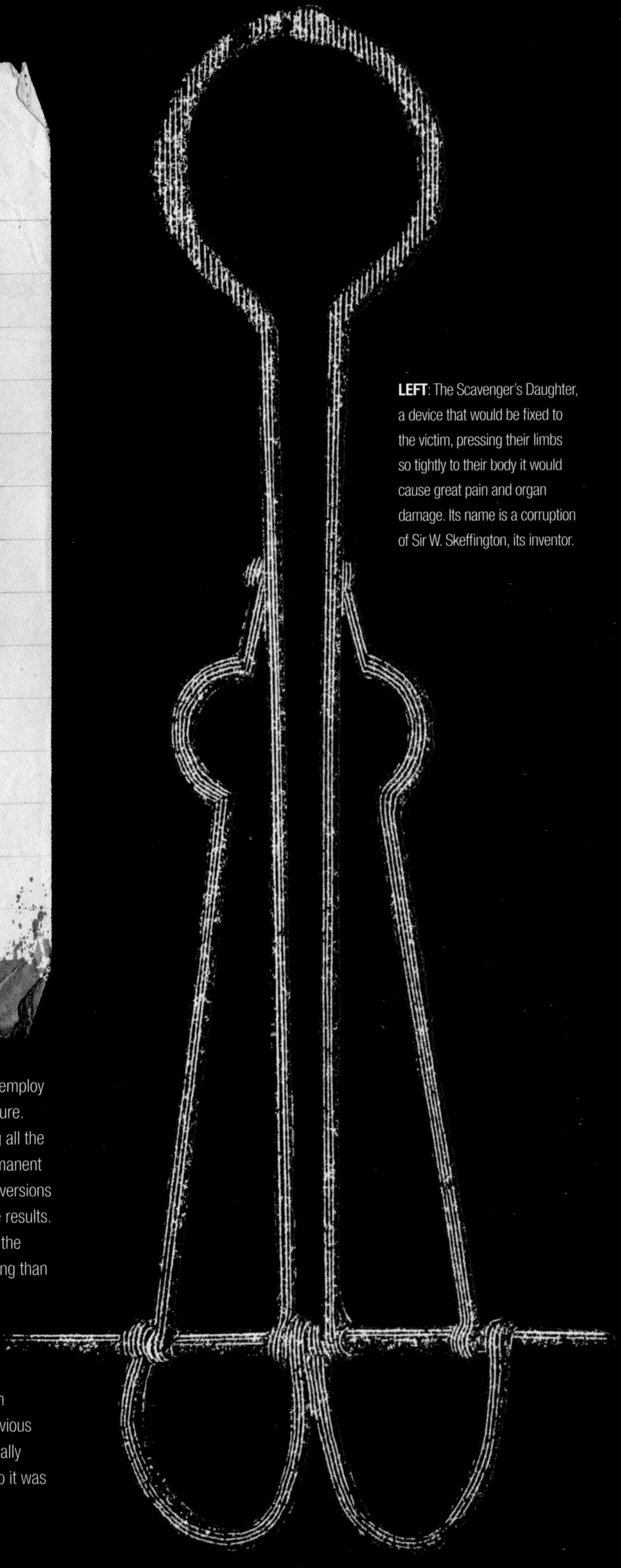

LEFT: The Scavenger's Daughter, a device that would be fixed to the victim, pressing their limbs so tightly to their body it would cause great pain and organ damage. Its name is a corruption of Sir W. Skeffington, its inventor.

If the torturer wanted merely to crush a victim's feet, then he could employ the "boot," which was fitted around the heel, sometimes made to measure. Wooden wedges were then hammered in until it closed tightly, crushing all the bones together. As with foot-whipping, the damage done would be permanent owing to the slow-healing nature of the small bones of the feet. Larger versions called brodequins were employed for the legs, with similarly destructive results.

A more precise device was the thumbscrews, a tiny vice into which the victim's digits were placed and which was then tightened. Less damaging than the other devices, it was therefore employed more frequently, both on the fingers and the toes, but there is little doubt it was still extremely painful and could cause permanent disability.

Essentially, any human body part could be crushed, either with rudimentary weights or with more precise devices, and if the victim survived, they could be left to heal and then worked over again, the previous damage causing even more pain. Full body crushing, however, was usually reserved for those who entirely refused to talk, and to submit yourself to it was seen by some as a form of perverse bravery.

WATER TORTURES

Among the common forms of torture which employed water were the ordeals mentioned in previous chapters (see pages 20–21), such as the ducking stool, or the forcing of the victim to place their hand in a pot of boiling water. However, there are a number of other water-related tortures which use different techniques. One in particular, waterboarding (see pages 58–59), has become increasingly popular (and controversial) in recent times, but was not so commonly used (in that form) in the past.

One technique that was used was to force-feed the victim large quantities of water, until they were bloated, filled to the brim. In seventeenth-century France, this was known as being "put to the question," with the amount differing from eight to 16 pints, depending on whether it was an ordinary or extraordinary question.

The nose might also be held closed with pincers or a clothes-peg. The water could be cold, or boiling, or adulterated in some way with waste matter

LEFT: Taken from a sixteenth-century woodcut, this image shows a victim being force-fed large quantities of water, as a clerk records his treatment and any possible confession.

BELOW: Sometimes a funnel or similar device would be used as a means to hold the throat open and bypass the victim's gag reflex as can be seen in this Japanese picture.

such as faeces and urine. When full, the subject would sometimes be turned onto their stomach to maximize the discomfort and pain. In some versions of the torture a board would be placed on the victim's stomach and two men would jump on it forcing mingled blood and water to jet from the mouth, nostrils, and ears.

Apart from the obvious pain, and irreparable internal damage to the throat and stomach, if the victim was not drained this type of punishment would eventually result in water intoxication. The consumption of too much water disturbs the balance of electrolytes in the body, leading to swelling in the brain, physical breakdown, kidney disorders, and eventually death.

Another way of using water to torture individuals was to soak them in cold water to increase the pain of whipping, and of other torture techniques that involve wounds on the skin, since the water softens the area. However, freezing water also numbs the body and could be seen as a form of relief or mercy, depending on when and how it was applied. If the water is mixed with some other liquid like vinegar, its application becomes more painful, while if it is adulterated with body fluids, the chances of infection increase.

Another way of using water to torture is to submerge individuals in it for a long time, but not necessarily to the point of drowning. Being in water for sustained periods can cause a number of painful health problems including full body sores, fungal infections, and gangrene, especially if the water is not clean, as would most likely have been the case.

Spontaneous water tortures include trapping the victim in a cave before the tide came in, which would then slowly fill with sea water. A more premeditated alternative would involve the creation of a water dungeon, a cell, or area in a prison which is filled with water. The most famous of these was perhaps the one in Amsterdam's Rasphuis, where the occupants would have to constantly work a pump at the center of the room to keep it from flooding and drowning them.

Individuals could be tortured with water by being pulled through it tied behind a fast-moving vessel, or by being keelhauled. The name of this punishment has become synonymous with pirates threatening each other, but it is often referenced without knowing the reality. The victim would be bound hand and foot, then thrown over the side of the ship and drawn by rope across either its width or length. Apart from the possibility of drowning, it is very likely serious injuries would occur from being dragged across the rough, splintered bottom of the vessel.

Ironically, one water torture was not actually giving any to the victim. A dearth of water could be obviously be ultimately as fatal as having too much.

LEFT: The Marquise De Brinvilliers was a noblewoman in seventeenth-century France who poisoned her father and brothers, and was forced to drink 16 pints of water during her captivity before being beheaded. This drawing depicts her on her way to be executed, following her torture by water.

BELOW: A lurid illustration of the torture of the Marquise De Brinvilliers, combined with her back being stretched by a rack-like device.

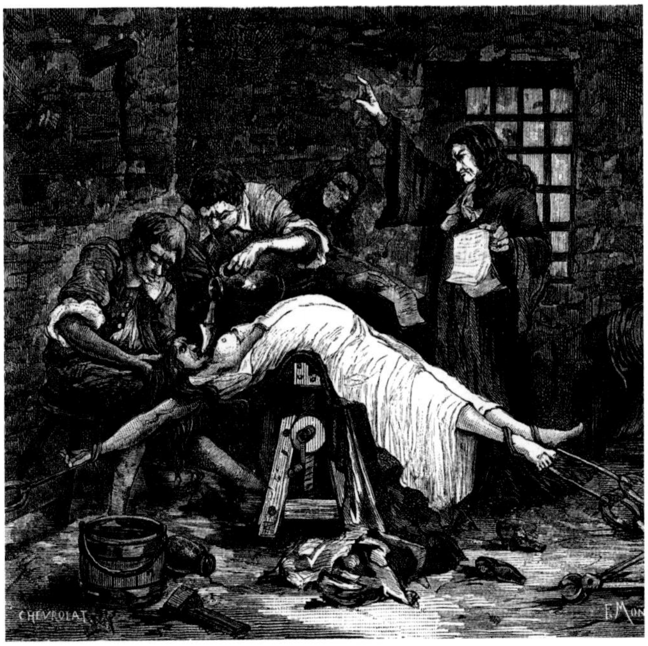

Dripping Water Torture

A mainly psychological torture technique, the dripping water torture was recorded, or perhaps invented, by Hippolytus De Marsiliis, a fifteenth-century Italian doctor and writer. Water would be dripped onto a secured prisoner's head, with changing frequency, sometimes rhythmic, sometimes not. This could continue for days until, supposedly, the victim would be driven insane with anticipation. Despite many apocryphal accounts attributing its employment to various countries, there are no solid accounts of its being used, so its effectiveness is unknown.

PIERCING

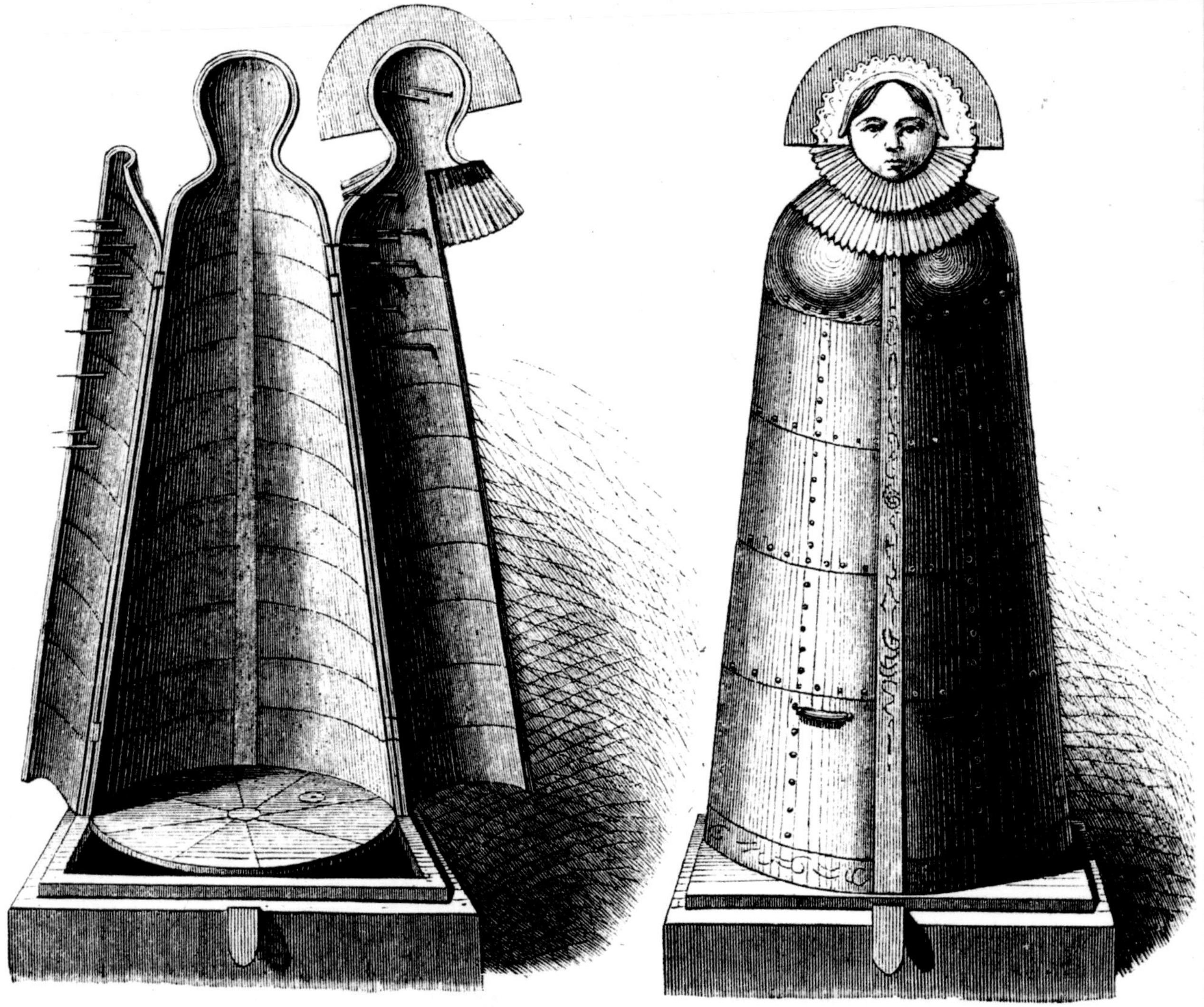

ABOVE: A woodcut dating from 1850 depiciting the legendary Iron Maiden.

While the vast majority of tortures depicted in this book have been well documented, with both physical evidence and accounts of their existence, some torture techniques and devices are less verifiable. Their existence may have been exaggerated or entirely fictionalized for dramatic purposes, to smear political enemies or simply through confusion between different sources. The trade in counterfeiting historical artifacts that grew from the eighteenth century onward further augmented these difficulties.

pre-dated the fourteenth century, while others claim it did not exist before the eighteenth century, which is when the device itself was reproduced out of a kind of macabre fascination. Whereas many torture devices are designed to produce slow torment, either to extract a confession or punish a transgression, there is something very quick and final about the Iron Maiden. Some accounts

The Apega of Nabis

This Spartan device is one of the most likely suspects as being the inspiration for the Iron Maiden. Nabis was a tyrannical Spartan king, and the iron Apega was supposedly built in the shape of his wife. It was a mechanical device with the arms and chest lined with spikes, dressed in clothes. Nabis would fool his victim into embracing it, then activate it and refuse to relent until they did what he asked, or he simply killed them for sport.

What historical piercing tortures may have led to the assumption of the Iron Maiden's medieval existence? One device known to have existed was the spiked barrel, a wooden barrel with metal spikes on the inside. The victim would be placed into this, usually naked, and rolled down a hill, with the velocity taking a horrific toll on their body. As well as its medieval use, this was a form of punishment employed by the ancient Romans.

An unusual device with a similar effect was called a cradle, a free-standing wooden box lined with spikes, with a semi-circle of wood at the bottom, so that once the victim was inserted, they could be rocked back and forth in a sinister parody of an actual cradle.

ABOVE: A Heretic's chair, complete with apparatus for crushing the ankles, exhibited with other medieval torture devices in St. Petersburg in Russia.

LEFT: A twentieth-century Hungarian postcard of Countess Elizabeth Báthory, who ruled over the area now known as Slovakia, and was thought to have tortured and murdered many people

While the Inquisition might not have used Iron Maidens, they may have used chairs lined with spikes, onto which the victim would be forced to sit. Surviving this was more likely than living through the Iron Maiden, but it would obviously cause horrific injury and victims may have died from blood loss or infection. In some devices, a small fire would be lit underneath the seat, making the spikes red-hot and even more painful and damaging.

Other common devices could be fitted with spikes. Captives would be made to wear metal collars or neck-braces lined with spikes, either as a form of punishment or a form of control. Similar devices named neck catchers were mounted on metal poles, so that the torturer could use them to move prisoners from one place to another.

There was also type of a chain with a series of tiny metal spikes or hooks called a cilice, but that was usually worn willingly, by someone wishing to undergo ritual punishment for religious purposes. Rumors persist that some groups wear them to this day, but the accuracy of these reports is, like the Iron

IMPALEMENT

One of the reasons for humanity's success as a species is its incredible resilience and ability to withstand trauma. It is therefore darkly ironic that so many tortures rely on that ability, to continue the pain for as long as possible, and to suspend the victim's body in horrifically unthinkable positions. This is the case with impalement.

The act essentially involved driving a long wooden or metal stake as far through the victim as possible. It could be inserted via the anus or genitalia, or into the side of the victim, hanging them sideways on it. Depending on the attention paid to the insertion, if the stake missed major organs, the victim could live for a long time; hours, and in some accounts (whose veracity is uncertain) even days. For this reason, a blunt stake was sometimes used. In seventeenth-century Denmark, the tradition was to insert the stake just under the skin, roughly where the spine was. That technique would make the victim's death even more prolonged. When pushed all the way through the body, the stake would sometimes emerge above the rib cage, and the end would be rested on the bottom of the jaw to prevent the victim sliding down the pole. As with other tortures there were many "creative" options for the torturer to consider.

The idea that one technique was more merciful than any other is ultimately misleading, as it would be an incredibly painful and horrifying experience in any variation. Like crucifixion (see pages 16–17), the combination of extreme physical trauma, being exposed to the elements (and insects) and any other humiliations or tortures that were performed on the victim would make this a particularly grueling experience. Impalement also shares with crucifixion a deliberate disregard for its victims, an indication that they were nothing but the lowest of animals.

Simple impalement was not the only form of this torture. Apart from the piercing types described in the previous chapter, there were other devices, like the Judas Cradle. This device was a chair, elevated a few feet from the ground, in which the seat was a pyramid-shaped piece of wood or metal. The victim would be placed onto this point, usually on a lower orifice, and secured either with rope or a metal belt. Then the torturer could apply weights to their arms or legs, subtly yet horrifically altering the effect of the spike driving itself into the body, or he could just let gravity take its course. Individuals could be suspended this way for longer than the other forms of impalement. However, as with the Iron Maiden, the reality of the Judas Cradle's employment has been brought into question. It could be a real medieval and Inquisition device, or the product of a macabre imagination that later became a reality.

Whether these two devices really existed or not, it remains the case that torture techniques that impaled bodily orifices in this manner were unpleasantly widespread. Even if the Inquisition did not use those particular devices, they had similar means at their disposal, employing wooden poles, hot irons or a horribly ornate device known either as an oral or anal Pear. This is a hand-held machine that resembles a metal flower. It would be inserted into one of the orifices, and by working the handle its "petals" would be driven outward, with obvious results. There is no doubt that being confronted in a torture chamber with any number of these devices would probably cause someone to confess immediately, but that was not really the ultimate goal. Impalement was, like crucifixion or the stocks, a way of putting the victim on display.

LEFT: A Judas Cradle, currently exhibited at the Museum of Medieval Torture, which is in Freiburg im Breisgau in Germany.

BELOW: A fifteenth-century German woodcut showing Vlad the Impaler callously dining surrounded by his victims.

RIGHT: A Mouth or Choke Pear, possibly used for body orifices other than the mouth.

Vlad Tepes (1531–76)

Vlad III, prince of Wallachia, became posthumously known as Vlad Tepes or Vlad the Impaler because of his predilection for that particular torture. A member of the Wallachian royal family during a particularly turbulent series of wars in the fifteenth century, Vlad III was at first placed on the throne by the Ottomans as a political move, but was deposed, only to reconquer his homeland nine years later. As part of his own war against the Ottomans, he is said to have impaled over 20,000 people in a "forest of stakes" to intimidate and insult the opposition.

WITCH HUNTS

While the various Inquisitions were ostensibly created to seek out and persecute those who contravened the doctrines of the Catholic Church, the many outbreaks of witch hunting throughout history have occurred under the banner of all sorts of different religions and societies. The most fervent and notable of these occurred mainly around Europe, from medieval times to the the early modern period (the fifteenth century onward), but the idea of witches and black magic seems to have always been with humanity.

If a village's crops were bad or its livestock fell sick for reasons that could not easily be explained, the inhabitants would blame some outside force. People were not stupid, but anger, frustration, and fear create a mob mentality and hysteria can easily sweep everyone up. Leading and feeding off these fears were the witchfinders.

As with the medieval inquisitions, the structure of the witch hunts differed from country to country and even from region to region. There was no single

BELOW: A girl is accused of being bedevilled at the witch trials in Salem, Massachusetts.

ABOVE: A lithograph of witches undergoing trial by water. It's very unlikely that any of those accused actually floated like the woman at the center.

massive crusade against witches, but instead a huge variety of different outbreaks. Despite this, there were certain elements which were constant. When suspicions grew in a village or town that someone was practicing witchcraft, and enough accusations had been circulated, those in charge would be asked to act, and often a witchfinder would descend on the area with his retinue and a trial would be conducted. This process would involve harsh interrogation of accusers, witnesses, victims, and their friends and family. The witchfinders were looking for various proofs, either in physical signs or behavior, such as those detailed in *Commentarius de Maleficius*, a book written by supposed demonologist Peter Binsfeld. Proofs included accounts of blasphemy, the witnessing of black magic ceremonies, diabolical marks, or, in many cases, a confession of forming a pact with the devil.

Various torture techniques were used, from trials of ordeal, to pressing and thumb screws, all designed to extract "the truth." Accusations would come thick and fast under this type of questioning, with the added pressure that supporting or just not incriminating the accused might cause the veil of suspicion to fall on anyone. Confessions also came "freely" under such a torture, if only to end it.

Some trials were conducted by people who thought themselves reasonable, and others were clearly orchestrated for the profit of the witchfinder and his assistants. For example, one way of testing a witch was the pricker, a metal needle with a handle, with which the suspect would be pricked to find a witch's mark, which is a spot that does not bleed. As witchfinder's profit and reputation depended on their success, some of them would use retractable needles to guarantee a result.

Once the victim was deemed to be guilty, there were a number of ways they might be executed. Burning at the stake is the most well known, but was not in fact the most frequent. It was more likely the condemned witch would be hung, though sometimes afterward their body would be burned anyway as an act of purification, to destroy any dark forces or demons that remained. The victim might also be beheaded with an axe or sword, or drowned during a trial of ordeal like the ducking stool. In some cases they might simply be exiled or mutilated, but this was less likely as the bible appeared to endorse death, saying in Exodus 22:18 that, "Thou shalt not suffer a witch to live."

Toward the end of the eighteenth century, witch hunts declined in popularity, having come under a wave of criticism from clergy and politicians both for their brutality and also for the non-Christian belief in magic and spirits that they implied. It is not certain how many died; estimates range from as few as 4,000 to over 63,000, mainly women, and inevitably all innocent, at least of witchcraft.

BELOW: Those convicted of witchcraft on their way to the gallows in chains, watched by a restless crowd.

Matthew Hopkins (ca.1619–47)

Matthew Hopkins is a mysterious figure, whose early history is largely undocumented, and yet for a period in the seventeenth century he was one of the most feared men in England as the self-proclaimed "Witchfinder General." He began hunting witches in 1645 and became hugely successful, using torture and fear and stirring communities up against each other as he used various texts and techniques to condemn the innocent. As his fame and cruelty grew the authorities felt he had overextended himself and society turned on him, after a witch hunting career lasting just 13 months.

BURNING AND BRANDING

The importance of fire both as a destructive force and as a metaphor for God's power has led to its use in a wide variety of tortures, such as the ordeals by fire used by the Inquisition (see pages 20–21 and 24–27), and the frying and roasting tortures (see pages 14–15) employed by the Romans. These uses persisted into the early modern era as well, but not necessarily in the way that is commonly thought. As mentioned in the previous chapter, while burning at the stake was considered by some to be the correct way to execute witches and many women were sentenced accordingly, whether their punishment was always carried out in quite this way out was another matter.

Another crime punishable at the time by burning at the stake was treason. But while high treason was a very strong accusation and usually reserved for those deliberately trying to kill or undermine the ruling classes, there also existed the crime of petty treason, which under common law was when someone murdered their direct superior. In particular, if a woman killed her husband, who was considered to be her master, she would be sentenced to burn at the stake. Something in the primal nature of this execution seems to suggest the sacrifices made to pagan gods in the past, to guarantee good crops and restore the balance upset by witchcraft or by something as unnatural as a wife raising her hand to her husband.

Catherine Hayes (executed 1726)

Catherine Hayes' life was fairly unexceptional by the standards of the time, poverty and social problems leading her to alternate between work as a maid and prostitution. During one of period of employment, she married her employer's son, but their relationship soured and she persuaded a lover to help her kill him. She was caught and sentenced to burn at the stake. As was usual, a cord was attached to hang her before the fire got too high, but it broke and she experienced the full horror of being burned alive.

Fire was not used simply to destroy someone totally, though, and the application of hot irons to the flesh of victims was another practice which extended into this period. Any part of the body could be mutilated in this way, following legal medieval practices, which persisted into early modern times, albeit under very different judicial circumstances.

There were many different types of brands, letters, and symbols, depending on the nature of the crime and which society was issuing the punishment. For example, in the middle of the sixteenth century those

LEFT: On the strength of false accusations, and from fear of an uprising, two black slaves are burned at the stake in eighteenth-century New York.

DOCUMENTS

ITEM 9: GILES COREY WARRANT AND SUMMONS

The warrant and summons for Giles Corey, the man crushed to death by pressing after refusing to enter a plea, as he did not recognise the Salem court's authority.

ITEM 10: EVIDENCE AGAINST SARAH WILDS

Evidence gathered against Sarah Wilds, who was also part of the Salem witch trials. She was convicted of witchcraft but escaped before being executed.

ITEM 11: ACCOUNT OF A SALEM JAIL KEEPER

The written account of a Salem jail keeper, showing those who were imprisoned or killed, and on which dates.

The deposition of Ann putnam Junr who testifieth and saith I have
ben afflected ever sence the begining of march with a woman that
tould me hir name was wildes and that she came from Topsfeild
but on the 22 April 1692 Sarah wilds did most greviously torment me
dureing the time of hir examination and then I saw that Sarah wilds
was that very woman that tould me hir name was wildes and also on
the day of hir examination I saw Sarah wilds or hir Appearance most
greviously torter and afflect mary walcott mircy lewes and Abigail william
and severall times sence Sarah wilds or hir Apperance has most
greviously tortored and afflected me with variety of torturs as by prick
-ing and pinching me and almost choaking me to death

Anne putnam Junr declared: ye above written: evidence: to be truth: before ye Jury of
inquest: June: 30th: 1692: upon oath

Salem 1692

The County of Essex is Dr to William Dounton Goale Keeper in Salem Decem the 1693.

To: Sarah Osburne 1 mo dyet in prison. Except 3s Recd in part — 0:07:0

To: Sarah Good 6 weekes and for her child Dorcas Good 1 mo dyet — 1:01:03

To: Giles Cory & his wife dyet 3 weeks remaines due there of — . 11. 03

To William Hobs 3 w. dyet — li . 07:06

To. Deliverance Hobs 12 months dyet — li 4:10.00

To: Abigail Hobs 12 mo dyet — li 4:10.00

To: Eliz Scargon 6 mo Dyet and for her child 4 mo Dyet — li 4:00:00

To: Alice parker 9 weekes dyet li 1: 00 00

To. Mary Toothaker 37 w dyet — li 3:07.00

To: Henr Salter 16 w: dyet — li 2:00:00

To: Rachel Hafield 10 w dyet — li 1:05:00

To: ye two Jacksons 4 weeks dyet Each li 1:00:00

To. Jno Hollen 4 W. dyet — li 0.10.00

To: Roger Wooland — li 3.00:

27:09:00

To: 9 years Salery at 5li p Anum agreed on & setled. out of wch only Recd 23li. Rest due 43:17:00

William Dounton — Allowed Wm Dounton for Salery since ye Revolution or Sr Edmd Andros Govmt wch might be due before his sd Governmt; in full — 12:11:00

40:00:00

Allowed

Salem Aprill the 18th 1692

There being Complaint this day made (Before us) by Ezekiell Cheever and John putnam Jun'r both of Salem Village Yeomen: in Behalfe of theire Majesties, for themselves and also for theire Neighbours against Giles Cory, and Mary Waren both of Salem farmes And Abigaile Hobs the daughter of Wm Hobs of the Towne of Topsfeild and Bridget Bishop the wife of Edw. Bishop of Salem Sawyer for high Suspition of Sundry acts of Witchcraft donne or Committed by them, upon the Bodys of: Ann putnam. Marcy Lewis, and Abig'l Williams and Mary Walcott & Eliz. Hubert of Salem Village whereby great hurt and dammage hath benne donne to the Bodys of said persons above named. therefore craved Justice

You are therefore in theire Majest's names hereby required to apprehend and bring before us Giles Cory & Mary Waren of Salem farmes, and Abigail Hobs the daughter of Wm Hobs of ye Towne of Topsfeild and Bridget Bishop ye wife of Edw. Bishop of Salem Tomorrow about Eight of the Clock in the forenoone, at ye house of Lt Nathaniell Ingersalls in Salem Village in order to theire Examination Relateing to the premises abovesd and hereof you are not to faile Dated Salem Aprill 18th 1692

To: George Herrick Marshall of the County of Essex —

John Hathorne
Jonathan. Corwin } Assis'ts

You are likewise required to Summons Margret Knight Lidya Nichols Elizabeth Nichols and Elizabeth Hubert Jonathan putnam and Hephzibah Rea all & every one of them to appeare before us at ye abovesd time & place to give in wt evidence they know Relateing to ye abovesd or like cases depending Dated Salem Aprill 18th 1692 —

18 ... 1692

I haue taken y^e within named persons and brought them to y^e house of Lef^t Nath: Ingersoll according to y^e tenner of y^e warrant p^r me Geo: Herrick Marshall of Essex

Aprill 18 = 1692

I haue sumonsd the within named persons to appeare att [illegible] and place within mentioned to Giue in whatt Euidence [illegible] Relateing to y^e premises p^r me Geo: Herrick

Marshall of Essex

Compl[illegible]

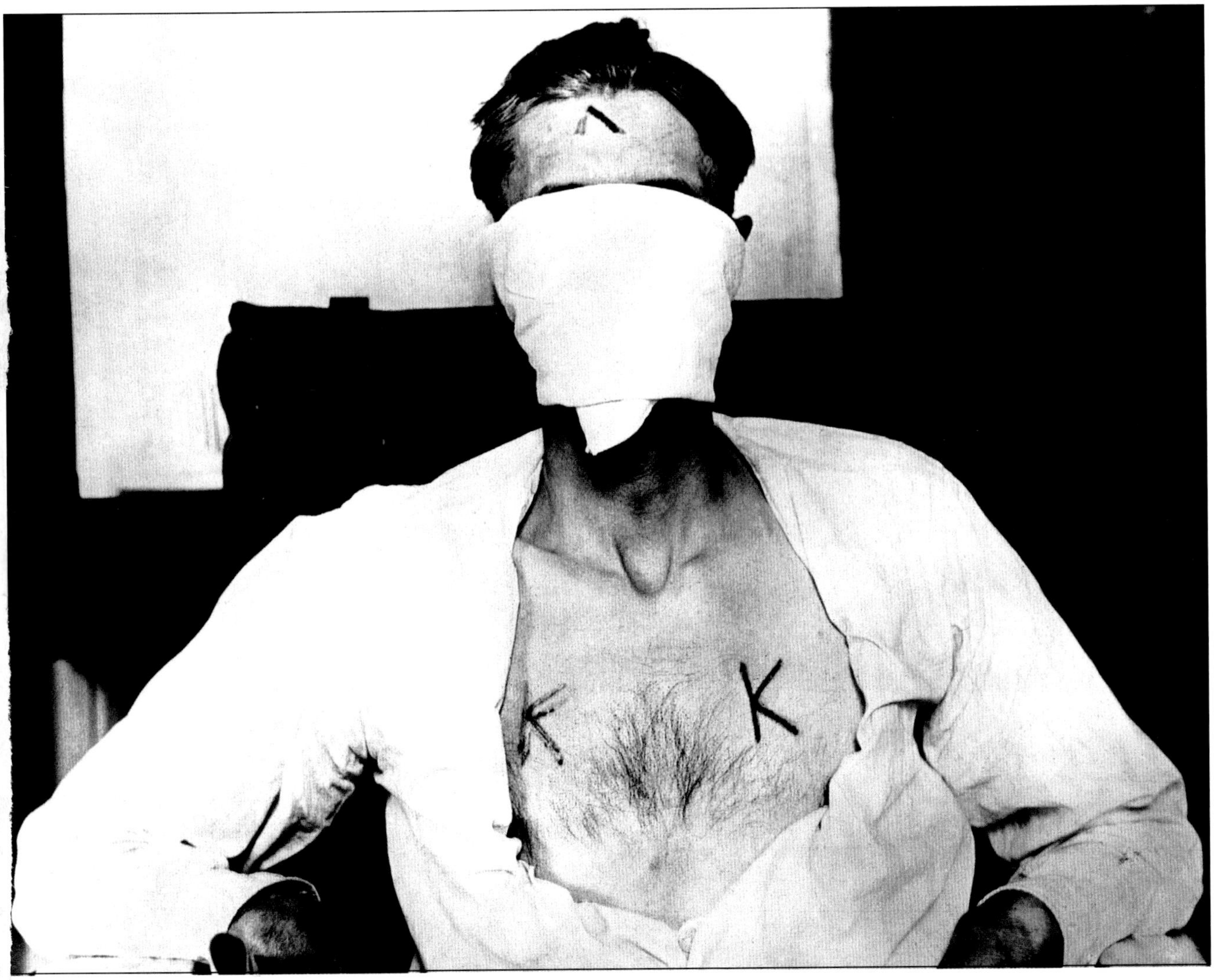

considered to be vagabonds would be marked with a "V" symbol on the chest. Those who blasphemed could have their foreheads burned with a "B," as well as having their tongues burned out.

Escaped slaves would be marked with an "S" on the face, usually on their cheeks. This would also help to identify them should they make another attempt at escape. Branding, aside from the punitive pain and mutilation, can therefore also be seen as an attempt to prevent crimes being committed in the future. Who would trust someone with an "M" for malefactor burned onto their body?

Branding has obvious connotations of ownership, as well (quite literally in the case of slaves). With criminals, there prevailed the idea that, by simply being criminals, they had thrown themselves onto the absolute power of the authorities, and every criminal was considered a certain potential repeat offender. There was no idea of rehabilitation; once you were branded with the mark you were a criminal for life.

There was also a religious application of branding, notably when the Anabaptists, an ultra-radical Protestant sect, were branded with cross shapes on their foreheads for refusing to return to the traditional mainstream of religion. Those who received these, as was the case with some others who received brands for crimes, bore their wounds with a perverse form of pride, as they considered themselves to be of the true faith. As fire represented destruction and also strange rebirth in the form of the phoenix, so brands transformed a human being into a living symbol of their own actions, for better or for worse.

ABOVE: Nelson Burroughs claimed that he was held captive by the Ku Klux Klan (KKK) for 17 days in 1924 and that during this time they burned Ks into his chest and forehead with a hot iron, in an attempt to get him to renounce Catholicism. Though he later said his story was a hoax, this form of punishment was in use at the time.

BELOW: A convict is branded on board a ship, possibly prior to transportation to another country.

FLOGGING

ABOVE: A man tied to a stake is publically whipped with a Cat o'nine tails at the Place Ste. Anne in Brazil while others awaiting the same fate cower in anticipation.

Despite the many developments in the types of torture used by humanity, some have always remained popular owing to their relative simplicity and capacity for inflicting pain. The use of whips for punishment, torture, and control, known as flogging or flagellation, seems to occur in all cultures and in most time periods. Only the types of whips and the rules for their use change. Their popularity seems second only to bladed weapons like knives and swords.

Whips, usually made of leather, but sometimes of tightly corded or tarred rope, can cause incredible damage to skin and open large welts or wounds in its surface. As the end of a whip is snapped by the wielder, the movement travels rapidly up its length, eventually attaining the speed of sound and creating a tiny sonic boom, which is the whip-crack noise (although to be properly audible the whip must have a "cracker" on the end). The noise itself can create great fear of what might come next, in both animals and humans.

In Europe, flogging was a punishment used for a wide variety of crimes, particularly those considered to be taking advantage of society's goodwill through theft or vagrancy. A public whipping was usually conducted by tying the victim to a whipping post (most towns or villages possessed one) and allowing people to jeer and then rub unpleasant substances like salt or mud into the wounds afterward. Despite this, the punishment was not intended to be fatal, but mercy was not really an option and the person doing the whipping sometimes lost control and killed the victim.

While a single-ended whip of various lengths, such as a bull whip or stock whip, was most commonly used, multiple-tailed whips could also be used in some circumstances. The most famous of these is the "Cat o' nine tails," a whip made of plaited cotton cord with nine ends or tails, which is best known for its employment by the British Royal Navy for a wide variety of crimes. Again, the punishment would be carried out with great ceremony in full view of the crew. It was also used by the British Army, and employed at penal colonies in various British-occupied countries. Ironically, despite its fame, the cat, as it was abbreviated, would be less painful than a leather whip, which was also sometimes used.

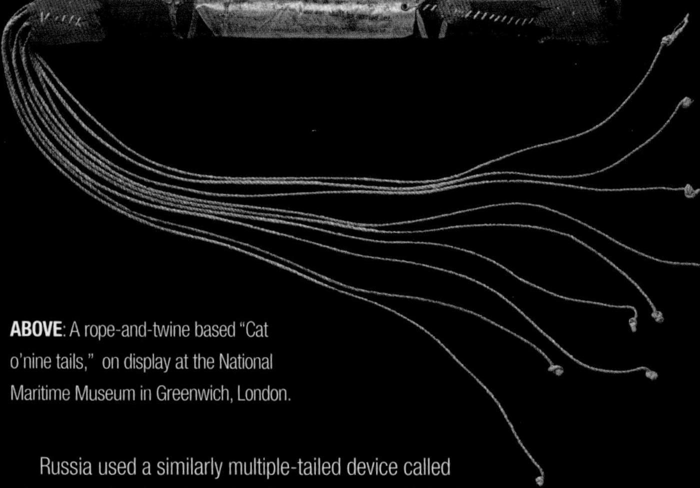

ABOVE: A rope-and-twine based "Cat o'nine tails," on display at the National Maritime Museum in Greenwich, London.

Russia used a similarly multiple-tailed device called a knout, made of leather rather than cotton, but this had an extra sadistic twist in that the ends would have metal hooks or wires attached to them to dig in to the skin. Sometimes these would be soaked in water and frozen, to increase the pain.

Another savage form of whip was the scourge, a multiple-tailed leather whip first favored by the Romans as a punishment for killing one's own parents, but later employed in Europe as the preferred weapon for punishing heretics. In a strange reversal, this whip became the tool of choice of the flagellants, a late medieval sect which practiced severe corporal mortification to show their dedication to the Lord and of what little worth they considered their physical bodies. They would ritually whip themselves each day in public until blood flowed and would encourage others to join them. This form of extreme masochism was also a reaction to the various natural disasters and plagues which occurred during the period, which some interpreted as God's punishment and a sign of the end of the world. By punishing themselves, the flagellants may have thought to mollify God. Whether this constitutes torture or not is up for debate, as it was self-inflicted, but those swept up in this form of mania may very well have found themselves in a position where refusal to participate would be very difficult.

The San Quentin Dungeon

San Quentin State Prison was established in July 1852, and its dungeon was finished in 1854, built by its own inmates. It was a notoriously cruel and unpleasant place to be incarcerated, packed with prisoners well beyond its supposed upper limit, with minimal sanitation. Waste buckets were kept open and uncovered in dark cold cells, where the prisoners slept on insect-riddled straw matting. Flogging with a water soaked rawhide strap was a frequent punishment for any prisoners guilty of transgression.

BELOW: A sailor is about to receive a flogging for a crime he did not commit so the real culprit steps forward as a point of honor, removing his shirt in anticipation of his own whipping.

WARTIME TORTURE

War is by its nature a brutal business, the act of attacking or defending entire communities or countries from enemy forces always leading to bloodshed and destruction, as well as shattered lives. In ancient or medieval wars, the torture of opponents was considered not just acceptable but expected, either to gather information, for punishment, or for sadistic pleasure. However, in the modern era, particularly from the late nineteenth century, the deliberate torture of prisoners (whether enemies or collaborators) became regarded as unacceptable. Early treaties such the Hague Conventions of 1899 and 1907, as well as the post-World War II Geneva Convention (1949), laid out protocols for what was permitted during periods of war, and torture itself became a war crime.

Of course, this did not put an end to it, and in fact very few successful prosecutions for specific cases of torture during World Wars I and Ii were undertaken, unless the torture formed part of some wider campaign of murder and persecution, such as the Holocaust.

During World War ii, Germany became notorious for its systematic use of torture and the threat of torture. This was used for a wide variety of reasons, such as extracting information from members of the anti-German resistance in occupied countries, or from prisoners of war. The effectiveness of this type of torture is still widely disputed. Torturers would be unlikely to have elaborate rooms full of equipment, but would instead restrain the victim in a cell or back room and use knives, beating with fists, some forms of water torture, and occasionally more complex techniques like squassation or burning with hot irons. These were not elaborate public displays, but formed part of the invisible machinery of oppression of the Nazi regime.

The treatment of prisoners of war differed from culture to culture and even from camp to camp, depending on those in charge. The poor treatment of prisoners arose from the belief that by being caught or even surrendering they had disgraced themselves and were therefore not deserving of mercy or even of being treated as human.

There is no question that the Nazis' persecution of the Jews and their creation and running of concentration camps was a form of mass torture. From the forced separation of families, to coercing the camp inmates into back-breaking work and starvation, it embraced acts of enormous cruelty.

This was compounded by doctors like Josef Mengele, who used the inmates of Auschwitz as test subjects for a series of cruel scientific experiments, from attempting to attach the body parts of one subject to another without permission

THIS PAGE BELOW AND FOLLOWING PAGE BELOW: Photographs of experiments carried out on a concentration camp inmate by German scientists. Here they test the effects of compression and decompression. This inmate was killed in an experiment.

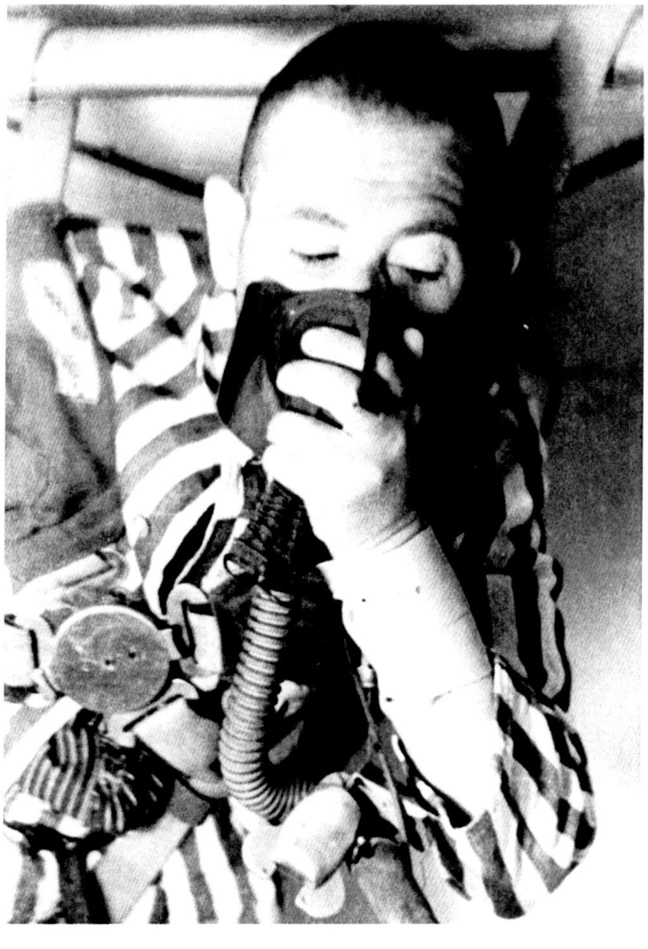

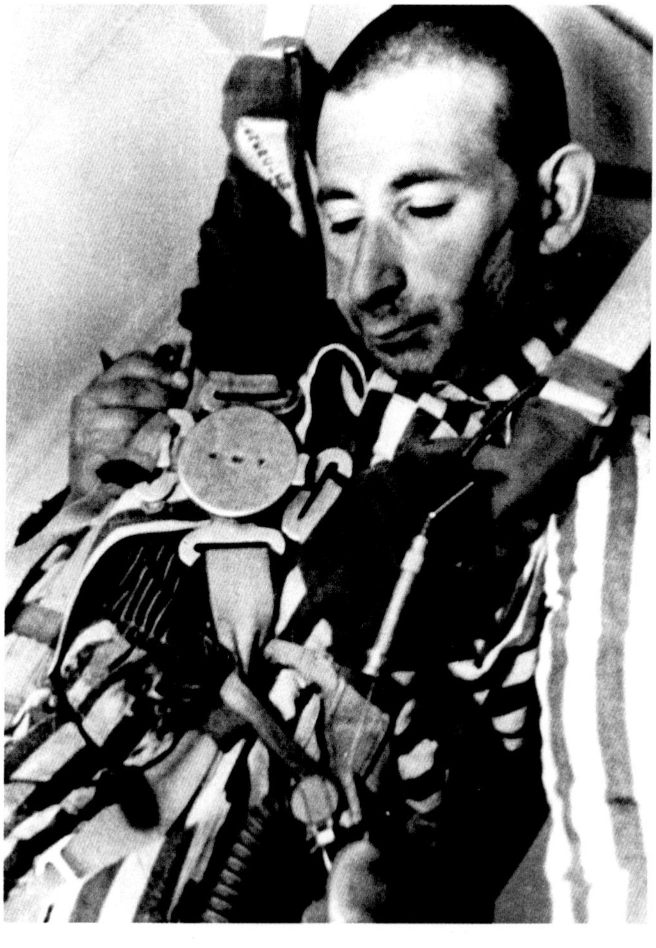

The Gestapo

The Geheime Staatspolizei, or Secret State Police, commonly abbreviated to Gestapo, was created in Germany in 1933 by splitting the intelligence and political departments from the regular police force. It was their job to investigate any sedition or dissent from within, and generally to control any opposition to the Nazi regime. To this end, they had enormous and unquestioned powers to inflict imprisonment or punishment. While they no doubt tortured many and terrorized even more, the Gestapo's true power came from the German public's complicity in its actions.

LEFT: Heinrich Müller, Chief of the Gestapo from 1939 until the end of the war.

or need, to injecting chemicals into children's eyes to change their color, as well as many occasions of surgery without anesthetic. It is not clear whether Mengele and others intended torture to cause pain or simply did not care.

Other countries such as Japan and the Soviet Union were known to use torture during these wars. The Soviet Union, although later to join the Allied side, refined torture almost to a science, and made liberal use of it. The Soviet leader Josef Stalin's paranoia about subversion from within as well as attack from without led him to treat all his citizens as if they were enemy agents. Starvation, sleep deprivation, and regular beatings were all part of the softening up technique that led to prisoners confessing and often selling out their friends and family.

Ultimately, every country at some point has used torture during a war. England, France, and the United States are not exceptions. In the Algerian War (1954–62) the French used squassation, mutilation, and electric shock torture on captured Muslim agents and those they suspected of harboring criminals, and similar techniques were used by other powers in the Korean (1950–53) and Vietnam Wars (1955–75).

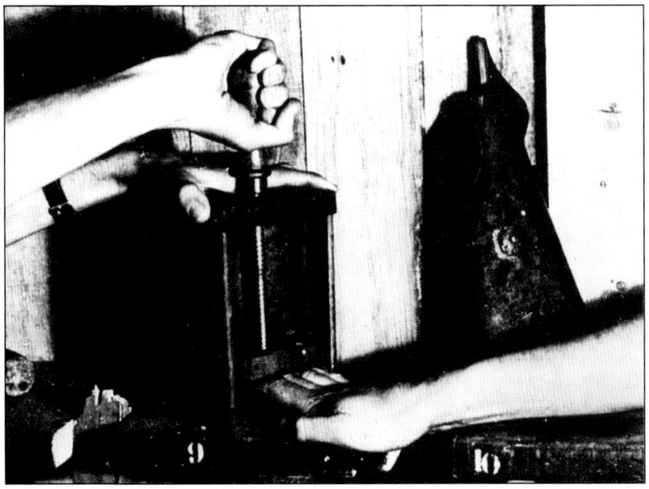

ABOVE: A hand-crushing device employed by the Gestapo on political prisoners.

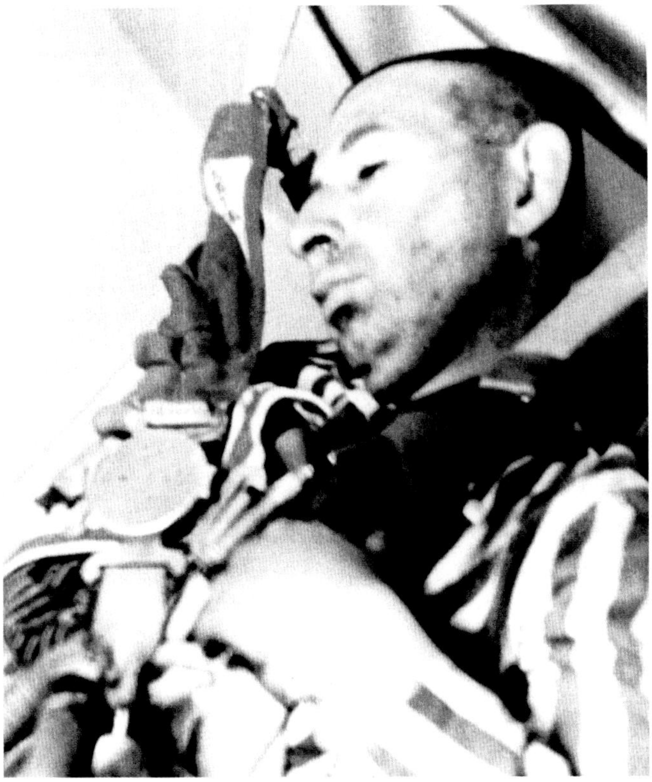

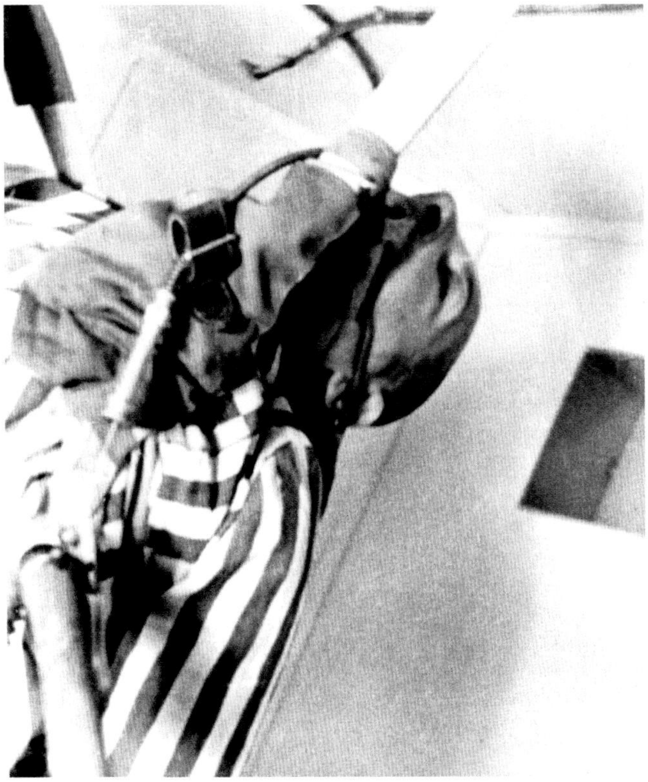

DRUGS AND PSYCHOCHEMICALS

ABOVE: The Headquarters of the Central Intelligence Agency (CIA) in Langley, Virginia, where some MKULTRA experiments were conducted.

Torture's effectiveness as a tool of intimidation and punishment is not just a result of the actual physical pain and damage it inflicts, but the impact of terror and uncertainty on the human mind. It therefore seems inevitable that torturers would turn to certain types of drugs to enhance and prolong the techniques that they use, in some situations, the administering of drugs becoming the torture itself.

In some cases the use of drugs was extremely primitive. In twentieth-century Brazil, torturers would inject alcohol directly onto the tongue, or other body parts, to induce incredible pain, and they later experimented with ether to similar effect. Alcohol or other numbing agents might be given to a tortured victim to increase their tolerance of pain, so they would last longer under conditions sober people might find unendurable.

Popular culture suggests that there is a truth drug, sometimes considered to be sodium pentothal, which, once administered, guarantees that the victim will spill any secrets immediately with no real ill effect. The truth is a lot more complex. There are drugs which can induce a form of hypnosis or a sedated state in the victim thus increasing their suggestibility, such as pentothal, sodium amytal, and substances like ethanol and hyoscine. Torturers could also attempt to influence the victim's mood by modulating between small quantities of stimulants like caffeine and relaxants like valium, trying to induce in the subject a disorienting "middle-state."

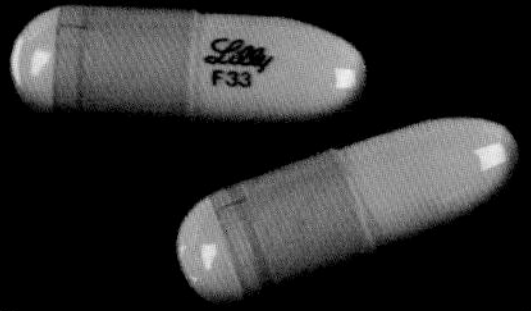

But even if this dreamlike reverie is achieved, there are no guarantees of the clarity of the victim's words, and they might be just as likely to fantasize and make facts up as ell the truth. Rumors have recently emerged of more effective ruth drugs in countries like Russia, but their existence is unproven and t could well be a politically motivated bluff to claim to possess such potent nterrogation tools.

The same techniques that put the victim into a shadowy uncertain state ould also be administered while they were being physically tortured, thereby rolonging their agony. With no clear sense of time passing, any pain could eem almost unending.

Most powerful nations have had programs designed to test the effectiveness of arious types of drugs and chemicals in the interrogation and control of prisoners. During World War II, Japan established the notorious Unit 731 military section hat performed human experimentation on thousands of innocent people, from horrific germ warfare tests to vivisection and disease exposure on a level almost omparable with the atrocities carried out by the Nazis.

A less horrific but still shocking series of experiments were conducted by he United States military in the MKULTRA program of the 1950s and 1960s s a reaction to allegedly similar programs conducted on American prisoners f war during the Korean War. The subjects were either government employees unaware they were being secretly administered drugs such as LSD and Mescaline, or members of the public tricked into involvement through special brothels or other fronts. Alongside drugs, other techniques such as sleep deprivation and hypnotism were used to see if the human mind could be programed to create secret assassins. The efforts were largely ineffective.

Another use of drugs within torture is to make it seem that the torture itself never took place. The secret police of many countries may wish to cover their tracks when interrogating suspects, and so by administering hallucinogenic or sedative drugs during or after torture, they could make the actual events that occurred uncertain to the victim, leaving them unable to describe them or incriminate their torturers.

Ultimately, while the effect of physical torture on the anatomy is largely understood because of centuries of torture experimentation, the effect of refined drugs on the human mind is still generally uncertain, and so their use for torture is far from widespread when compared to more simple but brutal methods.

ABOVE: Capsules of sodium amytal, which can have sedative and hypnotic properties.

BELOW: In 1975 President Ford personally met Frank Olson's family to apologize for Olson's suicide after he was given LSD without his knowledge.

Dr. Frank Olson (1901–53)

Frank Olson was an employee of the US Army in the area of microbiology, particularly biological warfare. He liaised with the MKULTRA program, formerly called Project Bluebird, and was probably complicit in some of its actions. He himself became a subject of the program when he was allegedly secretly given LSD by Dr. Sidney Gottlieb at a meeting with members of the project. The effects cannot be truly known but Dr. Olson suffered a nervous breakdown and less than a week later threw himself out of a tenth-floor window to his death.

ELECTRIC SHOCK TORTURE

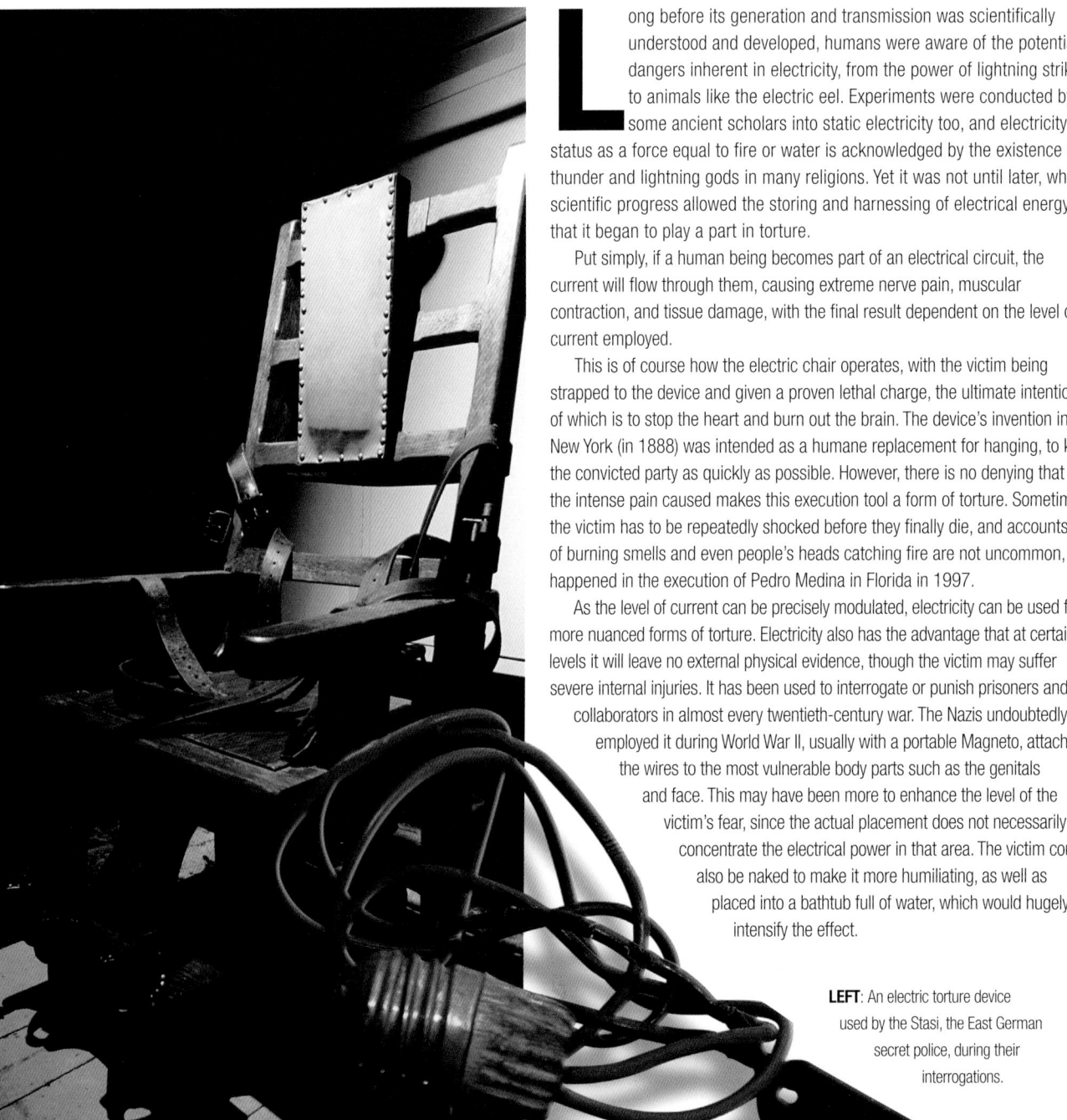

Long before its generation and transmission was scientifically understood and developed, humans were aware of the potential dangers inherent in electricity, from the power of lightning strikes to animals like the electric eel. Experiments were conducted by some ancient scholars into static electricity too, and electricity's status as a force equal to fire or water is acknowledged by the existence of thunder and lightning gods in many religions. Yet it was not until later, when scientific progress allowed the storing and harnessing of electrical energy, that it began to play a part in torture.

Put simply, if a human being becomes part of an electrical circuit, the current will flow through them, causing extreme nerve pain, muscular contraction, and tissue damage, with the final result dependent on the level of current employed.

This is of course how the electric chair operates, with the victim being strapped to the device and given a proven lethal charge, the ultimate intention of which is to stop the heart and burn out the brain. The device's invention in New York (in 1888) was intended as a humane replacement for hanging, to kill the convicted party as quickly as possible. However, there is no denying that the intense pain caused makes this execution tool a form of torture. Sometimes the victim has to be repeatedly shocked before they finally die, and accounts of burning smells and even people's heads catching fire are not uncommon, as happened in the execution of Pedro Medina in Florida in 1997.

As the level of current can be precisely modulated, electricity can be used for more nuanced forms of torture. Electricity also has the advantage that at certain levels it will leave no external physical evidence, though the victim may suffer severe internal injuries. It has been used to interrogate or punish prisoners and collaborators in almost every twentieth-century war. The Nazis undoubtedly employed it during World War II, usually with a portable Magneto, attaching the wires to the most vulnerable body parts such as the genitals and face. This may have been more to enhance the level of the victim's fear, since the actual placement does not necessarily concentrate the electrical power in that area. The victim could also be naked to make it more humiliating, as well as placed into a bathtub full of water, which would hugely intensify the effect.

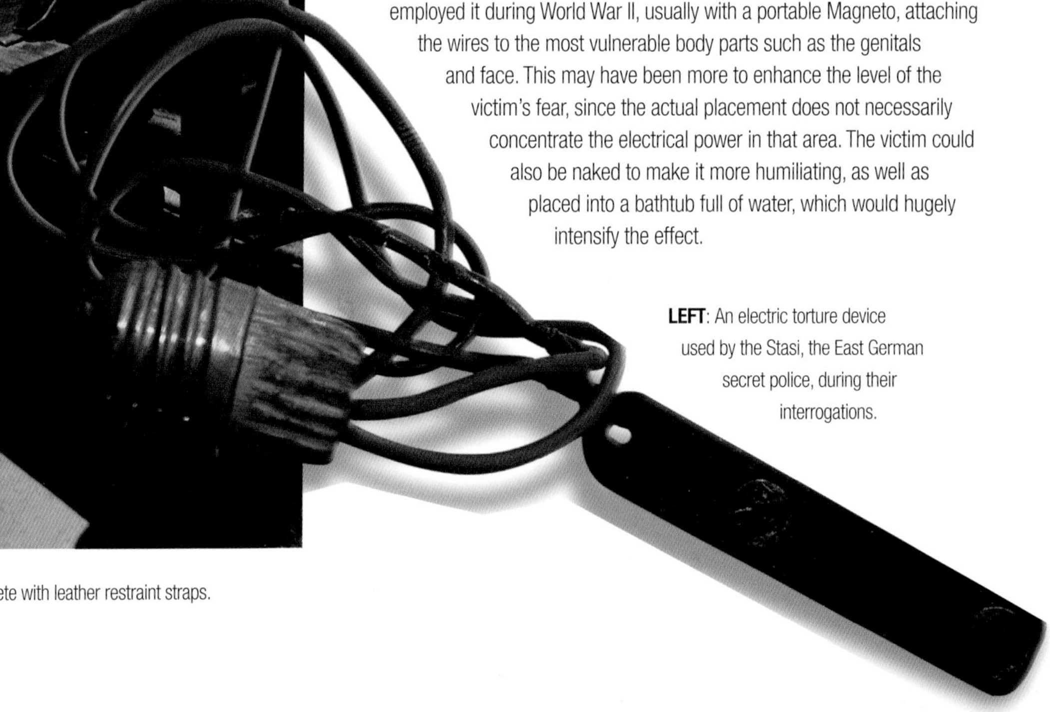

LEFT: An electric torture device used by the Stasi, the East German secret police, during their interrogations.

ABOVE: A decommissioned electric chair complete with leather restraint straps.

Tasers

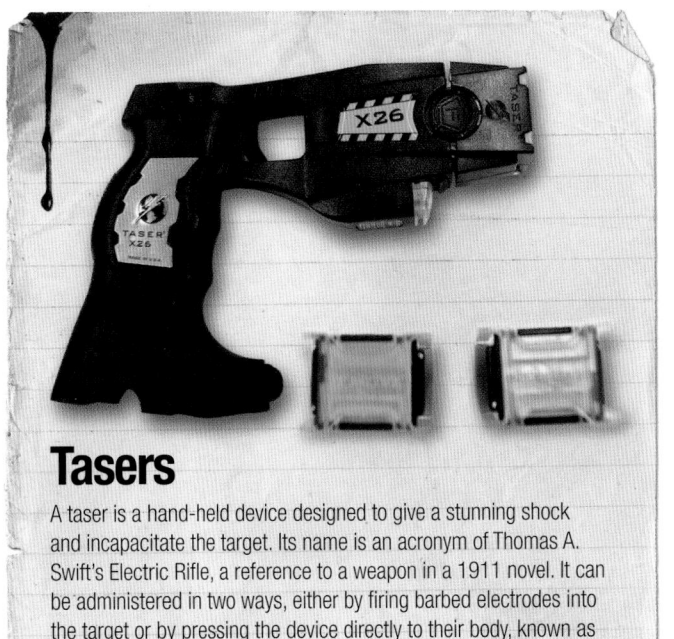

A taser is a hand-held device designed to give a stunning shock and incapacitate the target. Its name is an acronym of Thomas A. Swift's Electric Rifle, a reference to a weapon in a 1911 novel. It can be administered in two ways, either by firing barbed electrodes into the target or by pressing the device directly to their body, known as dry tasing. Though intended as a way to disable assailants with no permanent damage, reports of severe injuries and even death from the device have caused concerns about its deployment.

The Allies used electric torture during World War II, while both Americans and Vietnamese employed it in the Vietnam War. Russia also allegedly used such techniques during the conflicts in Chechnya from 1999.

At one time, the use of electricity was considered acceptable, as a humane form of torture, as the authorities in New York had hoped it would be as a method of execution. It is "pure pain" with no lasting physical side effects. Some countries consider it acceptable even now. However, medical studies have shown the notion of a damage-free torture to be simply untrue. Not just burns, but nerve damage can be permanent and brain function impeded. It is also worth mentioning that as the level of current is dictated by the torturer, should they be seized by any kind of passion or morbid sadism, they could easily set this at too high a level.

Interestingly, ECT or Electroconvulsive Therapy is used in hospitals as a controversial psychiatric treatment for those who suffer from mental disorders such as depression or anxiety. It has the effect of creating artificial seizures. The efficacy of this is disputed, and while the industry is now subject to some safeguards, in the past there have been numerous cases of this procedure being abused as a way of punishing wayward inmates. Whatever your viewpoint, the long-term effects of electric shocks on humans have yet to be fully revealed.

BELOW: A doctor administers electric shock and anaesthesia on a patient so that Dr. Walter Freeman can perform a trans-orbital lobotomy, a now discredited surgical technique wherein the surgeon uses a sharp instrument to sever the brain's connection to its frontal lobes.

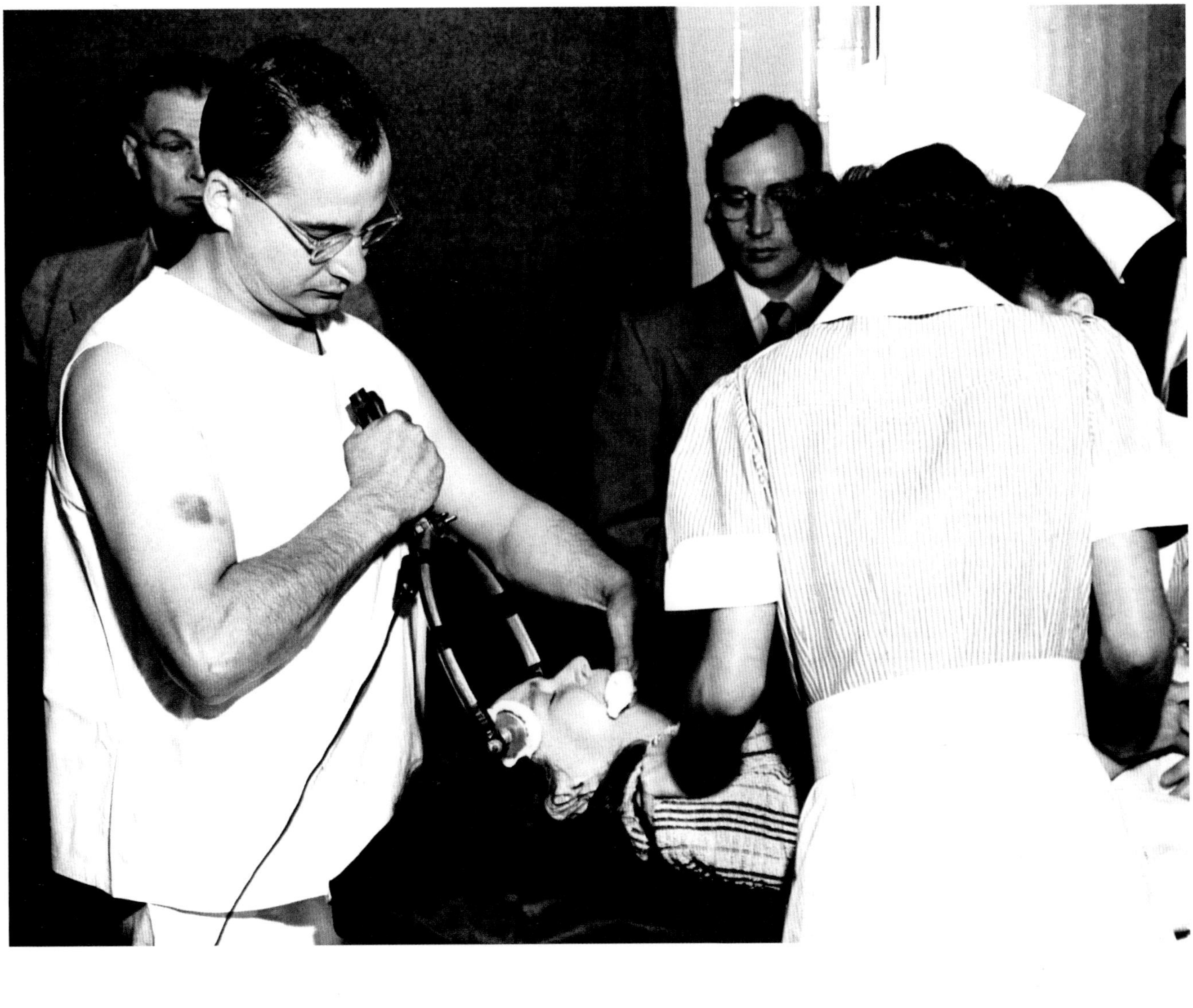

NECKLACING

ABOVE: A man is almost necklaced by an angry mob during a funeral after he is suspected of being a police informant. The tire was placed round his neck and filled with gasoline but a member of the clergy intervened before it could be lit.

While some tortures, like hanging or whipping, are common and have been used by many different cultures throughout history, others are more specifically bound to a time or place, and therefore loaded with social or political significance. This is the case with necklacing, an act strongly associated with the turmoil in South Africa in the 1980s and 1990s (although there have been more recent recurrences of the practice).

The act of necklacing is brutally simple. A rubber car tire filled with gasoline is forced onto a victim, either hung round their neck or pulled down, trapping their arms against their chest, and this is then set on fire. As the fire burns, it badly scorches the victim's body and the resultant fumes will cause them to choke and asphyxiate. Despite the incredible temperatures and poisonous gases, the victim can live for roughly half an hour in this state.

In the 1980s, South Africa's apartheid regime was notoriously cruel and oppressive, and was opposed directly by the African National Congress Party (ANC). Apart from socio-political action, the ANC also employed violence and sabotage against the government as a form of resistance. Often, those considered to have betrayed secrets or collaborated with the regime were innocent people just like during the inquisitions (see pages 24–27) and witch hunts (see pages 42–43) in previous eras. The ease of coming by rubber tires and gasoline further increased the popularity of necklacing as a form of execution. Friends and families of those accused might also be targeted.

The practice declined in the 1990s, especially once the apartheid system ended and the ANC came to power. However, there was a disturbing resurgence of it in 2008 after an influx of immigrants from other countries, mainly Zimbabwe led to widespread anti-immigrant violence when the newcomers were blamed for South Africa's economic hardships. There is no doubting the deliberate resonance of the use of that form of execution, in a way suggesting that immigrants were as much outsiders as those who collaborated with the apartheid regime.

This is not to say that necklacing is only practiced in South Africa. It has been reported in Nigeria, India, Sri Lanka, and in Brazil, where it is primarily used by members of drug syndicates and called *Microondas*, or "microwave oven." It also occurred in Haiti during the reign of the notorious Jean Claude "Papa Doc" Duvalier, as mobs targeted his supporters.

The results of necklacing are horrifying and in no way justified, whatever the supposed crime. Despite its employment of common twentieth-century items like artificial rubber car tires and refined petroleum, this mode of execution harks back to the mob practices of lynching or burning at the stake, which were ultimately an expression of anger and a form of malicious sadism, as well as a symbolic warning to others.

ABOVE: Winnie Mandela, then still the wife of the imprisoned Nelson Mandela, making a controversial speech in 1986 that implicitly endorsed the act of necklacing.

executed, and necklacing was the manner most often employed to carry this out. Its use was like a calling card to indicate who it was who had committed the murder, although officially the ANC condemned the practice. Some have suggested the association with the ANC was created and manipulated by their opponents in the apartheid government to stereotype them as vicious and bestial. In turn, there is no doubt that the techniques the apartheid regime itself employed to intimidate and control were also brutal and sadistic.

Necklacing was also sometimes used as part of the unofficial trials that villages or towns would set up to judge their own people, and thereby sidestep the official system set up by the apartheid government, which was naturally biased against black people. Nevertheless, it was not always employed "justly" and was often the result of an angry mob acting against anyone they considered to have transgressed, such as thieves or adulterers. Necklacing was sometimes even used against supposed witches, no doubt leading to the deaths of many

Desmond Tutu (1931–)

Archbishop Desmond Tutu is a South-African-born Anglican cleric and social campaigner. Educated in England, after being ordained as a priest he dedicated his life to fighting social and political injustice, particularly that of the apartheid regime. He remains a staunch Christian and has supported many liberal causes including that of gay rights. It is reported that in the 1980s he came across a crowd about to necklace someone, and pushed through to put his arms around the man to protect him, thereby saving his life.

PSYCHOLOGICAL TORTURE

The twentieth century has seen many advances in human society and one of these is an increasing abhorrence of the use of torture. Successive treaties and laws have been passed to eliminate its use worldwide, either in war or peace. Principal among these have been Article 3 of the Third Geneva Convention (1929), Article 5 of the Universal Declaration of Human Rights (1948), Article 3 of the Fourth Geneva Convention (1949), and the United Nations Convention Against Torture (1987). However, a result of this has been an increasingly creative embrace of techniques that, while not necessarily involving physical harm and pain, nonetheless cause the victim distress and psychological harm. Whether or not these actually constitute torture is an ongoing debate.

A commonly used technique is to deprive the captive of certain elements of life that are essential for normal functioning. Sleep deprivation has been employed as a component of interrogation and punishment by many modern countries, including Russian security agencies such as the NKVD and KGB, by the British Government (particularly in the 1970s), while it is still part of the US military's SERE (Survival, Evasion, Resistance, and Escape) program's techniques. Humans who have not slept for a number of days exhibit a wide range of physiological responses, from muscle aches and tremors, to memory loss and full-blown hallucinations. It magnifies the effect of any other duress they are under and can even increase the chances of developing diabetes.

Victims are kept awake by bombarding them with loud, unpleasant noise, and forced to stand in "stress positions" such as spreadeagled against a wall, or kept in hot, stifling conditions. However, whether or not someone in a sleep-deprived state is that useful to interrogators is often questioned, a dilemma similar to that involved with drugging prisoners.

BELOW: An inmate at Abu Ghraib prison in Iraq in 2003. Handcuffed semi-naked with a hood over his head, he was subject to a combination of humiliation and sensory deprivation.

DOCUMENTS

ITEMS 12 AND 13: VIETNAM POSTCARDS

Postcards created by US prisoners of war that were held at the Hanoi Hilton during the Vietnam War. It was a camp that used a wide variety of tortures including beatings, squassation, and long periods of solitary confinement, to break the wills of the prisoners.

ITEM 14: OBAMA EXECUTIVE ORDER

An Executive order signed by President Barack Obama in 2009 prohibiting the use of enhanced interrogation by US Officials, including waterboarding.

ITEM 15: UNIVERSAL DECLARATION OF HUMAN RIGHTS

The Universal Declaration of Human Rights, adopted by the United Nations General Assembly in 1948 as a proclamation that the signatory governments would dedicate themselves to greater equality and fair treatment for all human beings.

Sec. 6. *Construction with Other Laws.* Nothing in this order shall be construed to affect the obligations of officers, employees, and other agents of the United States Government to comply with all pertinent laws and treaties of the United States governing detention and interrogation, including but not limited to: the Fifth and Eighth Amendments to the United States Constitution; the Federal torture statute, 18 U.S.C. 2340–2340A; the War Crimes Act, 18 U.S.C. 2441; the Federal assault statute, 18 U.S.C. 113; the Federal maiming statute, 18 U.S.C. 114; the Federal "stalking" statute, 18 U.S.C. 2261A; articles 93, 124, 128, and 134 of the Uniform Code of Military Justice, 10 U.S.C. 893, 924, 928, and 934; section 1003 of the Detainee Treatment Act of 2005, 42 U.S.C. 2000dd; section 6(c) of the Military Commissions Act of 2006, Public Law 109–366; the Geneva Conventions; and the Convention Against Torture. Nothing in this order shall be construed to diminish any rights that any individual may have under these or other laws and treaties. This order is not intended to, and does not, create any right or benefit, substantive or procedural, enforceable at law or in equity against the United States, its departments, agencies, or other entities, its officers or employees, or any other person.

THE WHITE HOUSE,
January 22, 2009.

[FR Doc. E9–1885
Filed 1–26–09; 11:15 am]
Billing code 3195–W9–P

(a) **Establishment of Special Interagency Task Force.** There shall be established a Special Task Force on Interrogation and Transfer Policies (Special Task Force) to review interrogation and transfer policies.

(b) **Membership.** The Special Task Force shall consist of the following members, or their designees:

(i) the Attorney General, who shall serve as Chair;

(ii) the Director of National Intelligence, who shall serve as Co-Vice-Chair;

(iii) the Secretary of Defense, who shall serve as Co-Vice-Chair;

(iv) the Secretary of State;

(v) the Secretary of Homeland Security;

(vi) the Director of the Central Intelligence Agency;

(vii) the Chairman of the Joint Chiefs of Staff; and

(viii) other officers or full-time or permanent part-time employees of the United States, as determined by the Chair, with the concurrence of the head of the department or agency concerned.

(c) **Staff.** The Chair may designate officers and employees within the Department of Justice to serve as staff to support the Special Task Force. At the request of the Chair, officers and employees from other departments or agencies may serve on the Special Task Force with the concurrence of the head of the department or agency that employ such individuals. Such staff must be officers or full-time or permanent part-time employees of the United States. The Chair shall designate an officer or employee of the Department of Justice to serve as the Executive Secretary of the Special Task Force.

(d) **Operation.** The Chair shall convene meetings of the Special Task Force, determine its agenda, and direct its work. The Chair may establish and direct subgroups of the Special Task Force, consisting exclusively of members of the Special Task Force, to deal with particular subjects.

(e) **Mission.** The mission of the Special Task Force shall be:

(i) to study and evaluate whether the interrogation practices and techniques in Army Field Manual 2–22.3, when employed by departments or agencies outside the military, provide an appropriate means of acquiring the intelligence necessary to protect the Nation, and, if warranted, to recommend any additional or different guidance for other departments or agencies; and

(ii) to study and evaluate the practices of transferring individuals to other nations in order to ensure that such practices comply with the domestic laws, international obligations, and policies of the United States and do not result in the transfer of individuals to other nations to face torture or otherwise for the purpose, or with the effect, of undermining or circumventing the commitments or obligations of the United States to ensure the humane treatment of individuals in its custody or control.

(f) **Administration.** The Special Task Force shall be established for administrative purposes within the Department of Justice and the Department of Justice shall, to the extent permitted by law and subject to the availability of appropriations, provide administrative support and funding for the Special Task Force.

(g) **Recommendations.** The Special Task Force shall provide a report to the President, through the Assistant to the President for National Security Affairs and the Counsel to the President, on the matters set forth in subsection (d) within 180 days of the date of this order, unless the Chair determines that an extension is necessary.

(h) **Termination.** The Chair shall terminate the Special Task Force upon the completion of its duties.

Sec. 3. *Standards and Practices for Interrogation of Individuals in the Custody or Control of the United States in Armed Conflicts.*

(a) **Common Article 3 Standards as a Minimum Baseline.** Consistent with the requirements of the Federal torture statute, 18 U.S.C. 2340–2340A, section 1003 of the Detainee Treatment Act of 2005, 42 U.S.C. 2000dd, the Convention Against Torture, Common Article 3, and other laws regulating the treatment and interrogation of individuals detained in any armed conflict, such persons shall in all circumstances be treated humanely and shall not be subjected to violence to life and person (including murder of all kinds, mutilation, cruel treatment, and torture), nor to outrages upon personal dignity (including humiliating and degrading treatment), whenever such individuals are in the custody or under the effective control of an officer, employee, or other agent of the United States Government or detained within a facility owned, operated, or controlled by a department or agency of the United States.

(b) **Interrogation Techniques and Interrogation-Related Treatment.** Effective immediately, an individual in the custody or under the effective control of an officer, employee, or other agent of the United States Government, or detained within a facility owned, operated, or controlled by a department or agency of the United States, in any armed conflict, shall not be subjected to any interrogation technique or approach, or any treatment related to interrogation, that is not authorized by and listed in Army Field Manual 2–22.3 (Manual). Interrogation techniques, approaches, and treatments described in the Manual shall be implemented strictly in accord with the principles, processes, conditions, and limitations the Manual prescribes. Where processes required by the Manual, such as a requirement of approval by specified Department of Defense officials, are inapposite to a department or an agency other than the Department of Defense, such a department or agency shall use processes that are substantially equivalent to the processes the Manual prescribes for the Department of Defense. Nothing in this section shall preclude the Federal Bureau of Investigation, or other Federal law enforcement agencies, from continuing to use authorized, non-coercive techniques of interrogation that are designed to elicit voluntary statements and do not involve the use of force, threats, or promises.

(c) **Interpretations of Common Article 3 and the Army Field Manual.** From this day forward, unless the Attorney General with appropriate consultation provides further guidance, officers, employees, and other agents of the United States Government may, in conducting interrogations, act in reliance upon Army Field Manual 2–22.3, but may not, in conducting interrogations, rely upon any interpretation of the law governing interrogation—including interpretations of Federal criminal laws, the Convention Against Torture, Common Article 3, Army Field Manual 2–22.3, and its predecessor document, Army Field Manual 34–52—issued by the Department of Justice between September 11, 2001, and January 20, 2009.

Sec. 4. *Prohibition of Certain Detention Facilities, and Red Cross Access to Detained Individuals.*

(a) **CIA Detention.** The CIA shall close as expeditiously as possible any detention facilities that it currently operates and shall not operate any such detention facility in the future.

(b) **International Committee of the Red Cross Access to Detained Individuals.** All departments and agencies of the Federal Government shall provide the International Committee of the Red Cross with notification of, and timely access to, any individual detained in any armed conflict in the custody or under the effective control of an officer, employee, or other agent of the United States Government or detained within a facility owned, operated, or controlled by a department or agency of the United States Government, consistent with Department of Defense regulations and policies.

Sec. 5. *Special Interagency Task Force on Interrogation and Transfer Policies.*

Federal Register
Vol. 74, No. 16
Tuesday, January 27, 2009

Presidential Documents

Title 3—

The President

Executive Order 13491 of January 22, 2009

Ensuring Lawful Interrogations

By the authority vested in me by the Constitution and the laws of the United States of America, in order to improve the effectiveness of human intelligence-gathering, to promote the safe, lawful, and humane treatment of individuals in United States custody and of United States personnel who are detained in armed conflicts, to ensure compliance with the treaty obligations of the United States, including the Geneva Conventions, and to take care that the laws of the United States are faithfully executed, I hereby order as follows:

Section 1. *Revocation.* Executive Order 13440 of July 20, 2007, is revoked. All executive directives, orders, and regulations inconsistent with this order, including but not limited to those issued to or by the Central Intelligence Agency (CIA) from September 11, 2001, to January 20, 2009, concerning detention or the interrogation of detained individuals, are revoked to the extent of their inconsistency with this order. Heads of departments and agencies shall take all necessary steps to ensure that all directives, orders, and regulations of their respective departments or agencies are consistent with this order. Upon request, the Attorney General shall provide guidance about which directives, orders, and regulations are inconsistent with this order.

Sec. 2. *Definitions.* As used in this order:

(a) "Army Field Manual 2–22.3" means FM 2–22.3, Human Intelligence Collector Operations, issued by the Department of the Army on September 6, 2006.

(b) "Army Field Manual 34–52" means FM 34–52, Intelligence Interrogation, issued by the Department of the Army on May 8, 1987.

(c) "Common Article 3" means Article 3 of each of the Geneva Conventions.

(d) "Convention Against Torture" means the Convention Against Torture and Other Cruel, Inhuman or Degrading Treatment or Punishment, December 10, 1984, 1465 U.N.T.S. 85, S. Treaty Doc. No. 100–20 (1988).

(e) "Geneva Conventions" means:

(i) the Convention for the Amelioration of the Condition of the Wounded and Sick in Armed Forces in the Field, August 12, 1949 (6 UST 3114);

(ii) the Convention for the Amelioration of the Condition of Wounded, Sick and Shipwrecked Members of Armed Forces at Sea, August 12, 1949 (6 UST 3217);

(iii) the Convention Relative to the Treatment of Prisoners of War, August 12, 1949 (6 UST 3316); and

(iv) the Convention Relative to the Protection of Civilian Persons in Time of War, August 12, 1949 (6 UST 3516).

(f) "Treated humanely," "violence to life and person," "murder of all kinds," "mutilation," "cruel treatment," "torture," "outrages upon personal dignity," and "humiliating and degrading treatment" refer to, and have the same meaning as, those same terms in Common Article 3.

(g) The terms "detention facilities" and "detention facility" in section 4(a) of this order do not refer to facilities used only to hold people on a short-term, transitory basis.

Federal Register

Tuesday,

January 27, 2009

Part V

The President

Executive Order 13491—Ensuring Lawful Interrogations

Executive Order 13492—Review and Disposition of Individuals Detained at the Guantánamo Bay Naval Base and Closure of Detention Facilities

Executive Order 13493—Review of Detention Policy Options

THE UNIVERSAL DECLARATION OF Human Rights

WHEREAS *recognition of the inherent dignity and of the equal and inalienable rights of all members of the human family is the foundation of freedom, justice and peace in the world,*

WHEREAS *disregard and contempt for human rights have resulted in barbarous acts which have outraged the conscience of mankind, and the advent of a world in which human beings shall enjoy freedom of speech and belief and freedom from fear and want has been proclaimed as the highest aspiration of the common people,*

WHEREAS *it is essential, if man is not to be compelled to have recourse, as a last resort, to rebellion against tyranny and oppression, that human rights should be protected by the rule of law,*

WHEREAS *it is essential to promote the development of friendly relations among nations,*

WHEREAS *the peoples of the United Nations have in the Charter reaffirmed their faith in fundamental human rights, in the dignity and worth of the human person and in the equal rights of men and women and have determined to promote social progress and better standards of life in larger freedom,*

WHEREAS *Member States have pledged themselves to achieve, in co-operation with the United Nations, the promotion of universal respect for and observance of human rights and fundamental freedoms,*

WHEREAS *a common understanding of these rights and freedoms is of the greatest importance for the full realisation of this pledge,*

NOW THEREFORE THE GENERAL ASSEMBLY

PROCLAIMS *this Universal Declaration of Human Rights as a common standard of achievement for all peoples and all nations, to the end that every individual and every organ of society, keeping this Declaration constantly in mind, shall strive by teaching and education to promote respect for these rights and freedoms and by progressive measures, national and international, to secure their universal and effective recognition and observance, both among the peoples of Member States themselves and among the peoples of territories under their jurisdiction.*

ARTICLE 1 —All human beings are born free and equal in dignity and rights. They are endowed with reason and conscience and should act towards one another in a spirit of brotherhood.

ARTICLE 2 —1. Everyone is entitled to all the rights and freedoms set forth in this Declaration, without distinction of any kind, such as race, colour, sex, language, religion, political or other opinion, national or social origin, property, birth or other status.

2. Furthermore, no distinction shall be made on the basis of the political, jurisdictional or international status of the country or territory to which a person belongs, whether this territory be an independent, Trust or Non-Self-Governing territory, or under any other limitation of sovereignty.

ARTICLE 3 —Everyone has the right to life, liberty and the security of person.

ARTICLE 4 —No one shall be held in slavery or servitude; slavery and the slave trade shall be prohibited in all their forms.

ARTICLE 5 —No one shall be subjected to torture or to cruel, inhuman or degrading treatment or punishment.

ARTICLE 6 —Everyone has the right to recognition everywhere as a person before the law.

ARTICLE 7 —All are equal before the law and are entitled without any discrimination to equal protection of the law. All are entitled to equal protection against any discrimination in violation of this Declaration and against any incitement to such discrimination.

ARTICLE 8 —Everyone has the right to an effective remedy by the competent national tribunals for acts violating the fundamental rights granted him by the constitution or by law.

ARTICLE 9 —No one shall be subjected to arbitrary arrest, detention or exile.

ARTICLE 10 —Everyone is entitled in full equality to a fair and public hearing by an independent and impartial tribunal, in the determination of his rights and obligations and of any criminal charge against him.

ARTICLE 11 —1. Everyone charged with a penal offence has the right to be presumed innocent until proved guilty according to law in a public trial at which he has had all the guarantees necessary for his defence.

2. No one shall be held guilty of any penal offence on account of any act or omission which did not constitute a penal offence, under national or international law, at the time when it was committed. Nor shall a heavier penalty be imposed than the one that was applicable at the time the penal offence was committed.

ARTICLE 12 —No one shall be subjected to arbitrary interference with his privacy, family, home or correspondence, nor to attacks upon his honour and reputation. Everyone has the right to the protection of the law against such interference or attacks.

ARTICLE 13 —1. Everyone has the right to freedom of movement and residence within the borders of each state.

2. Everyone has the right to leave any country, including his own, and to return to his country.

ARTICLE 14 —1. Everyone has the right to seek and to enjoy in other countries asylum from persecution.

2. This right may not be invoked in the case of prosecutions genuinely arising from non-political crimes or from acts contrary to the purposes and principles of the United Nations.

ARTICLE 15 —1. Everyone has the right to a nationality.

2. No one shall be arbitrarily deprived of his nationality nor denied the right to change his nationality.

ARTICLE 16 —1. Men and women of full age, without any limitation due to race, nationality or religion, have the right to marry and to found a family. They are entitled to equal rights as to marriage, during marriage and at its dissolution.

2. Marriage shall be entered into only with the free and full consent of the intending spouses.

3. The family is the natural and fundamental group unit of society and is entitled to protection by society and the State.

ARTICLE 17 —1. Everyone has the right to own property alone as well as in association with others.

2. No one shall be arbitrarily deprived of his property.

ARTICLE 18 —Everyone has the right to freedom of thought, conscience and religion; this right includes freedom to change his religion or belief, and freedom, either alone or in community with others and in public or private, to manifest his religion or belief in teaching, practice, worship and observance.

ARTICLE 19 —Everyone has the right to freedom of opinion and expression; this right includes freedom to hold opinions without interference and to seek, receive and impart information and ideas through any media and regardless of frontiers.

ARTICLE 20 —1. Everyone has the right to freedom of peaceful assembly and association.

2. No one may be compelled to belong to an association.

ARTICLE 21 —1. Everyone has the right to take part in the government of his country, directly or through freely chosen representatives.

2. Everyone has the right of equal access to public service in his country.

3. The will of the people shall be the basis of the authority of government; this will shall be expressed in periodic and genuine elections which shall be by universal and equal suffrage and shall be held by secret vote or by equivalent free voting procedures.

ARTICLE 22 —Everyone, as a member of society, has the right to social security and is entitled to realisation, through national effort and international co-operation and in accordance with the organisation and resources of each State, of the economic, social and cultural rights indispensable for his dignity and the free development of his personality.

ARTICLE 23 —1. Everyone has the right to work, to free choice of employment, to just and favourable conditions of work and to protection against unemployment.

2. Everyone, without any discrimination, has the right to equal pay for equal work.

3. Everyone who works has the right to just and favourable remuneration insuring for himself and his family an existence worthy of human dignity, and supplemented, if necessary, by other means of social protection.

4. Everyone has the right to form and to join trade unions for the protection of his interests.

ARTICLE 24 —Everyone has the right to rest and leisure, including reasonable limitation of working hours and periodic holidays with pay.

ARTICLE 25 —1. Everyone has the right to a standard of living adequate for the health and well-being of himself and of his family, including food, clothing, housing and medical care and necessary social services, and the right to security in the event of unemployment, sickness, disability, widowhood, old age or other lack of livelihood in circumstances beyond his control.

2. Motherhood and childhood are entitled to special care and assistance. All children, whether born in or out of wedlock, shall enjoy the same social protection.

ARTICLE 26 —1. Everyone has the right to education. Education shall be free, at least in the elementary and fundamental stages. Elementary education shall be compulsory. Technical and professional education shall be made generally available and higher education shall be equally accessible to all on the basis of merit.

2. Education shall be directed to the full development of the human personality and to the strengthening of respect for human rights and fundamental freedoms. It shall promote understanding, tolerance and friendship among all nations, racial or religious groups, and shall further the activities of the United Nations for the maintenance of peace.

3. Parents have a prior right to choose the kind of education that shall be given to their children.

ARTICLE 27 —1. Everyone has the right freely to participate in the cultural life of the community, to enjoy the arts and to share in scientific advancement and its benefits.

2. Everyone has the right to the protection of the moral and material interests resulting from any scientific, literary or artistic production of which he is the author.

ARTICLE 28 —Everyone is entitled to a social and international order in which the rights and freedoms set forth in this Declaration can be fully realized.

ARTICLE 29 —1. Everyone has duties to the community in which alone the free and full development of his personality is possible.

2. In the exercise of his rights and freedoms, everyone shall be subject only to such limitations as are determined by law solely for the purpose of securing due recognition and respect for the rights and freedoms of others and of meeting the just requirements of morality, public order and the general welfare in a democratic society.

3. These rights and freedoms may in no case be exercised contrary to the purposes and principles of the United Nations.

ARTICLE 30 —Nothing in this Declaration may be interpreted as implying for any State, group or person any right to engage in any activity or to perform any act aimed at the destruction of any of the rights and freedoms set forth herein.

UNITED NATIONS

Adopted by the United Nations General Assembly at its 183rd meeting held in Paris on 10 December 1948

Issued by U.N. Department of Public Information

IHT_ITEM 15

Rape

While sexual assault is undoubtedly a physical form of torture, its lasting effects are mainly psychological, though saying this is not to diminish its horrifying effect. Its use in both war and "ethnic cleansing" and by oppressive regimes as a form of weapon is sadly widespread. From the Japanese army in World War II forcing captives to become prostitutes or "comfort women," to the horrific mass rapes of Tutsi women during the Rwandan Genocide of 1994, it has cast a terrible shadow over the whole of human history.

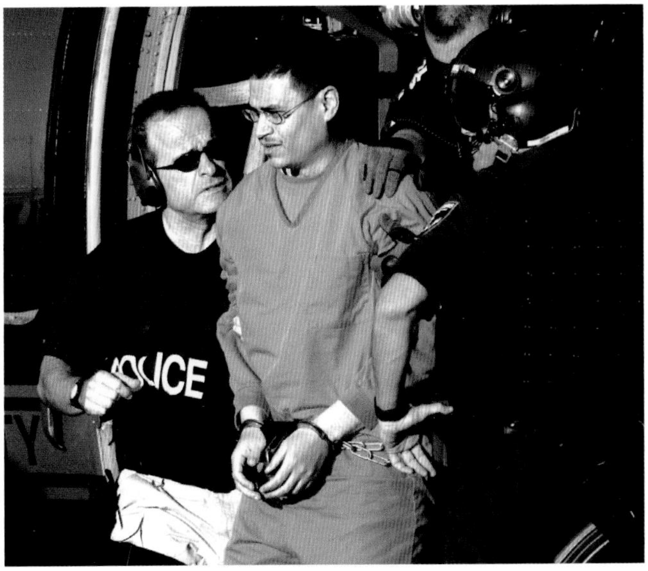

RIGHT: José Padilla in 2006 being escorted by police to Miami federal court to face terrorism charges in a civilian court after his status as an enemy combatant was rescinded.

Another necessary element of human life is social contact, and solitary confinement is a punishment that totally removes that. In prisons, those put in solitary are generally either being punished for rule-breaking or are considered dangerous to the populace, but their confinement is usually for a limited period.

Extended periods of solitary confinement, sometimes years, have been used to break down the will of captives, leading them to lose all sense of time and space and their own existence. Sometimes they are kept entirely in the dark, or hooded and restrained, as in the US military detention center at Guantanamo Bay.

This practice can cross the line into total sensory deprivation, which is even more disorienting and potentially deranging. José Padilla, a Guantanamo inmate, who was later convicted of aiding terrorists, was kept in a room with no natural light, clocks or any other stimuli, and when moved outside wore opaque goggles and headphones. Eventually, he began to suffer mental side-effects and believed that everyone was colluding in his captivity, even his lawyers and family members.

Another technique is the mock execution. Making someone believe they are about to die can cause great stress on the mind, especially if it happens several times, with the effect compounding itself, providing the victim is convinced of his tormentor's dangerous nature and sincerity. Stalin was particularly fond of this technique, often ordering his opponents (whether real or imagined) to be subjected to it, and as he was just as fond of ordering thousands of people be killed on a whim, the victim would be unlikely to think the execution fake until the last minute.

Of course, one of the most vicious and effective psychological tortures is to threaten the victim's loved ones. Again, if this is asserted with enough realism, the thoughts of those the victims care about being hurt, or even simply ruined financially or ostracized, can be enough to cause them considerable anguish.

Ultimately, are these kinds of psychological techniques torture or simply "enhanced interrogation"? Opinions differ, but studies show they have very real physical effects and make a permanent impact.

BELOW: Many people suffer from ophidiophobia or fear of snakes. Vietnamese torturers would sometimes leave one or more non-poisonous snakes in a cell overnight with a captive to induce fear and panic.

WATERBOARDING

ABOVE: Anti-war activists demonstrate waterboarding during a protest outside the White House in 2009.

In some people's estimations waterboarding, also known as mock drowning, should not be in this book at all. The debate over its significance and morality has raged for almost half a decade, and looks set to continue, despite that in January 2009 President Barack Obama banned its use by United States personnel.

There are different techniques, but each generally involves the victim being bound hand and foot to a wooden board which is sloped backward. Cloth is placed over the victim's face and soaked in water until it clings, blocking the mouth and nose, at which point a great deal of water is channeled onto the head for about 30 or 40 seconds, simulating the sensation of drowning. During one session, this procedure may be performed dozens of times. The victim experiences a sense of choking and panic, as well as pain and the activation of the gag reflex, further impeding breathing.

This is not an entirely modern invention, and was first practiced by the Spanish Inquisition. It was also used by the Japanese Army and the Gestapo during World War II, and by the Khmer Rouge in Cambodia in the 1970s. But its most recent controversial application was by US troops in Iraq, and on the terrorism suspects held at the American military camp at Guantanamo Bay in Cuba.

The argument is that as waterboarding does not technically involve actual drowning, it is only a psychological strain that is placed on the victim, and therefore does not constitute torture. It is regarded instead as an "enhanced interrogation technique," part of a series of authorized methods of treating

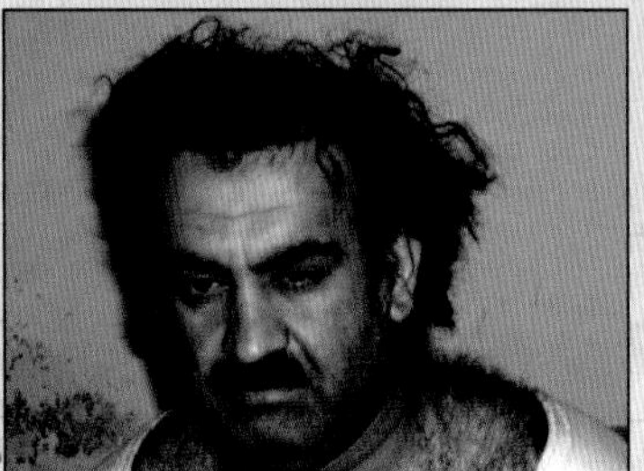

Khalid Sheik Mohammed (1964–)

Khalid Sheik Mohammed was a high-ranking member of Al Qaeda, and is currently imprisoned in Guantanamo Bay, having been moved there in 2006 from a secret facility. In 2008, the CIA said that they had performed waterboarding on him and he had confessed to involvement in many terrorist activities including the 9/11 plane attacks on the World Trade Center. He was said to have given information that had helped capture several other Al Qaeda members and possibly foil future attacks. He later disputed this, saying he had supplied false information to get his interrogators to stop.

prisoners, which also includes most psychological tortures, as well as physical techniques such as slapping and being kept in a freezing room.

Whether or not the sensation is psychological or physiological depends on how it is conducted. If gallons of water are poured over the victim's head, this will be much closer to actual choking and drowning than if the water is slowly and carefully applied. There is also the issue of whether or not the victim is aware of what is happening. If the process is explained to them, it is said that it will have less of an impact than if it is performed on them without explanation.

However, accounts from those subjected to the procedure seem to say that even if the victim knows that they are not actually being drowned, it still feels like it, affecting the body at an instinctive level. Indeed, those who undergo the procedure have been known to struggle so hard that they can actually fracture their limbs.

Some of those who claim waterboarding is not torture have undergone the procedure to prove it is not as traumatic an experience as is believed. These experiments have had differing results. When writer Christopher Hitchens was subjected to it, he had those administering it stop after a very short time, changing his mind entirely about waterboarding, as did talk show host Erich Muller.

Others argue that, although it may be a form of torture, the use of waterboarding and other techniques are entirely necessary in what they term the "ticking time bomb" scenario: if a terrorist or group of terrorists had secretly set up a time bomb somewhere in the world, and the only way to learn its location and how to disarm it was torture, surely its use would be justified? It is up to each person's conscience to decide, but unlike its portrayal in film and television, torture has never been shown to be a very effective way of getting useful information.

Although torture and its use is officially banned in many countries, some governments have used "extraordinary rendition" to ship suspects to other places where they could be tortured to gather information.

Ultimately, as with all the tortures in this book, all the different reasons and justifications people give for its use, you have to look at who else has used and is using the techniques, and ask if that is really the company you wish to keep.

BELOW: A Viet Cong captive is tortured by an American First Air Cavalryman and a Vietnamese interpreter with an impromptu form of waterboarding using a towel and a canteen.

FURTHER READING

Books:

Diehl, Daniel, and Mark P. Donnelly. *The Big Book of Pain: Torture and Punishment Through History*. UK: The History Press, 2008.

Greenberg, Karen Joy. *The Torture Debate in America*. UK: Cambridge University Press, 2005.

Horvitz, Leslie Alan, and Christopher Catherwood. *Encyclopedia of War Crimes and Genocide*. UK: Facts on File, 2006.

Miejer, Fik, and Liz Waters. *The Gladiators: History's Most Deadly Sport*. UK: Souvenir Press, 2004.

Peters, Edward. *Torture*. US: University of Pennsylvania Press, 1996.

Previté-Orton, Charles William. *The Shorter Cambridge Medieval History*. UK: Oxford University Press, 1991.

Scott, George Ryley. *A History of Torture*. UK: Sphere, 1971.

Starr, Chester G. *A History of the Ancient World*. UK: Oxford University Press, 1991.

Vacandard, Elphege. *The Inquisition: A Critical and Historical Study of the Coercive Power of the Church*. US: Catholic Author's Press, 2006.

Whiting, Roger. *Crime and Punishment: A Study Across Time*. UK: Nelson Thornes Ltd, 1986.

Websites:

Salem Witch Trials Documentary Archive and Transcription Project:
http://etext.virginia.edu/salem/witchcraft

The Peabody Essex Museum:
http://www.pem.org

The Edgar Allan Poe Museum:
http://www.poemuseum.org/index.php

NOTABLE DUNGEONS, TORTURE CHAMBERS, AND MUSEUMS

The Hoa Lo Prison aka Hanoi Hilton, Vietnam

Used as a Vietcong POW Camp, this facility was partly demolished but what remains houses a small museum on its history.

Tower of London, UK

The Tower is more properly called Her Majesty's Royal Palace and Fortress and operated as a prison for almost 900 years. It has many interesting displays and exhibits about its dark history.
http://www.hrp.org.uk/toweroflondon

The London Dungeons, UK

More of a tourist attraction than a serious museum, it is nonetheless very frank and informative about the torture and punishment in London's history. There are also dungeons operated by the same company located at York in the UK, Edinburgh in Scotland, Hamburg in Germany, and Amsterdam in Holland.
http://www.thedungeons.com

Palace of the Inquisition, Cartagena, Colombia

Ilt was once a center of the Inquisition's activity, but now this ancient building is a museum as well as a memorial to its victims.

Salem, Massachussetts, USA

Not the only place the witch hunts occurred in the USA, but probably the best known, Salem has many well preserved buildings from the time and history themed tours.
http://www.salemwitchmuseum.com

Daliborka Tower, Prague Castle/ Prague Torture Museum, Czech Republic

Daliborka Tower, part of Prague Castle, was formerly a prison and torture facility, and now houses an exhibition about its history. The city also has a well regarded torture museum nearby.

Templo Mayor, Mexico City, Mexico

An archeological dig site unearthing one of the main temples of the capital of the Aztec nation. Evidence of hundreds of human sacrifices has been discovered in the area as well as many torture techniques.

Alcatraz Island, San Francisco, USA

The famous prison is now a popular tourist attraction, with regular tours conducted by former guards telling stories of its inmates and harsh environment.
http://www.nps.gov/alca/index.htm

National Museum of Crime and Punishment, Washington D.C., USA

Well researched and with a great number of exhibits, this museum is not restricted to torture and punishment but also covers crime and techniques used to fight it in the past and today.
http://www.crimemuseum.org

Museum of Historic Torture Devices, Wisconsin Dells, USA

While not as high profile as the Washington equivalent, this museum nonetheless has a considerable collection of torture devices and methods.
http://www.dellstorturemuseum.com

The Medieval Torture Museum, San Gimignano, Italy

The large collection on display here is also sometimes taken on tour to other parts of Italy and even other countries, as part of a campaign against the continuing use of some of the devices in parts of the world.
http://www.torturamuseum.com/this.html

The Torture Museum, Amsterdam, Holland

A small, dark museum which displays a number of old prints alongside its collection of torture equipment.
http://www.amsterdam.info/museums/torture-museum

INDEX

ENTRIES IN ITALICS DENOTE AN ILLUSTRATION

A

Abu Ghraib *56*
adultery 15, 23
African practices *15*, 54–55
Al Qaeda 58
alcohol 50
American practices *44*, *45*, 56, 58–59
anatomy, study of 33
ANC (African National Congress) 54–55
ancient cultures 6–10, *11*, 14, 15, *15*, 16–19, *32*, 39, 44
animals, torture involving 18–19, 51
see also insects
anti-immigrant violence 55
apartheid regime 54–55
Apega of Nabis 39
Assyrian practices 10
Aztec practices 10, *11*

B

Babalonian practices 9, 20
barrel pillory 13
barrel, spiked 39
bastinado (foot whipping) 7
Bàthory, Elizabeth 38, *39*
beating 6–7
beheading 22, 31, 43
bestiarii 18
biblical references 11, 14, 43
Binsfield, Peter 42
Blood Countess 38, *39*
Bloody Assizes 23, *23*
boats, the see *scaphism*
boiling 14–15
Bonfire of the Vanities 29
boots 35
branding 44–45, 48
Brazen Bull of Phalaris 15, *15*
Brazilian practices 27, *46*, 50, 55
breaking 30–31
breaking wheel 31, *31*
British (English) practices 30, 56
brodequins 35
burning 44–45
burning at the stake 21, *24*, 43, 44, *44*

C

Caligula, Emperor *32*
Cambodian practices 58
castration 8
Cat o' nine tails 46, *47*
Cathars 24
Catherine wheel 31
Catholic Church 16, 24–27, 35, 42
CIA *50*
cilice 39
circumcision 8–9
college hazing 6
Colosseum, the 19
Colombian neck-tie 32
conventions against torture 56
Corey, Giles 34, *34*
cradle, spiked 39
criminal punishments 7, 9, 20–21, 45
crucifixion 13, 16–17, *16*, 28, 40
crushing 34–35, *49*
cutting 32–33
Cyrus the Younger 13

D

Danish practices 40
De Brinvilliers, Marquise *37*
death, torture after 9, 10, 22, 31
disease, deliberate exposure to 51
disembowelling 22–23, *22*
drawing (disembowelling and emasculating) 22–23, *22*
dripping water torture 37
drowning 58–59
see also water tortures
drug barons, torture by 32, 55
drugs as torture 50–51
drunkard's cloak 13
ducking stool *20*, 36, 43

E

Egyptian practices 6, 7, 8, 9
electric chair 52, *52*
electric shock torture 49, 52–53
enhanced interrogation techniques 57, 58
Episcopal Inquisition 24
ether 50
ethnic cleansing 57
European practices *9*, 18–27, 34–35, 36, 42, 46
executions, mock 57
experimentation on victims 48–49, *48–49*, 51
falaka (foot whipping) 7
Fawkes, Guy 31, *31*
fire tortures 20, 39, 43, 44–45, 54–55
fire, trial by 20–21, *20*
flagellants 47
flagellation *see flogging*
flaying 10–11, 32
flogging 46–47, *46*
see also whipping
food, torture using 14–15
foot whipping (bastinado) 7
Ford, President *51*

F

frying 14–15
Galvarino *9*
gang initiation 6
gasoline (necklacing) 54
gauntlet, running the 21

G

Geneva Conventions 48, 56
germ warfare tests 51
Gestapo 49, 58
gladiators 18–19
Greek practices 10, *11*, 14, 15, *15*, 16
Guantanamo Bay 57, 58

H

Hague Conventions 48
Haiti 55
Hammurabi, Code of 9, *9*, 20
hanging 22–23, 43
hanging, drawing, and quartering 22–23
Hannah and seven sons 14
Hayes, Catherine 44, *44*
hazing 6
heresy 24–25, 31, 39, 47
Heretics Chair *39*
Holocaust 48
Hopkins, Matthew 43, *43*
Hugh Despenser the Younger *22*, 23

I

impalement 17, 40–41
Indian practices 27, 55
inquisitions 24–27, 29, 30, 38, 40, 44, 55, 58
insects, torture using 12–13, *13*, 17, 40
Iraq war 56, 58
Iron Maiden 38, *38*, 39
iron virgin 38
Islamic punishments 8

J

Japanese practices 51, 57, 58
Jesus Christ 17, *17*
Jewish persecution 14, 27, 48
Joan of Arc 21, *21*
Judaic punishments 8
Judas Cradle 40, *40*

K

keelhauling 37
Khmer Rouge 58
Klu Klux Klan *45*
knout 47

L

lobotomy 53
loved ones, threats to 57
LSD 51

M

Machiavelli, Niccolò 28, *28*
Mandela, Winnie *55*
Marsyas 10, 11
Medici 28–29
Mengele, Josef 48–49
Microondas 55
medieval practices 20–21, 23, 34, 38–39, 42
Middle Ages 20–21, 23, 34, 38–39, 42
Mithridates 13, *13*
MKULTRA program *50*, 51
mock drowning 58–59
mock executions 57
Mohammed, Khalid Sheik *58*
Moriscos 27
Müller, Heinrich *49*
mutilation 8–9, 28, 32, 49

N

Native American practices 11, 13
Nazi practices 48
neck catcher 29
necklacing 54–55
Nero, Emperor 15
Norse practices 16

O

Obama, President Barack 58
Olson, Dr Frank 51
ordeal, trial by 20–21, 24

P

Padilla, Jose 57, *57*
pear, anal 40
Pear, Mouth or Choke 40, *41*
pendulum 33, 33
persecution, religious 14, 15, 16–17, *19*, 24–27
Persian practices 12, 13, 16, *33*
phalanga (foot whipping) 7
Phalaris, Brazen Bull of 15, *15*
piercing 38–39
pillory 8, *8*, 13
Portuguese Inquisition 27